Pretty Evil

PENNSYLVANIA

PENNSYLVANIA

TRUE STORIES OF MOBSTER MOLLS, VIOLENT VIXENS, AND MURDEROUS MATRIARCHS

STEPHANIE HOOVER

Globe
Pequot

GUILFORD, CONNECTICUT

Globe Pequot

An imprint Globe Pequot, the trade division of The Rowman & Littlefield Publishing Group, Inc.
4501 Forbes Blvd., Ste. 200
Lanham, MD 20706
www.rowman.com

Distributed by NATIONAL BOOK NETWORK

Copyright © 2021 by Stephanie Hoover

British Library Cataloguing in Publication Information available

Library of Congress Cataloging-in-Publication Data

Names: Hoover, Stephanie, author.
Title: Pretty evil Pennsylvania : true stories of mobster molls, violent
    vixens, and murderous matriarchs / Stephanie Hoover.
Description: Lanham, MD : Globe Pequot, [2021] | Identifiers: LCCN 2021032087 (print) | LCCN
    2021032088 (ebook) | ISBN
    9781493055029 (paperback) | ISBN 9781493055036 (epub)
Subjects: LCSH: Murder—Pennsylvania—Case studies. | Women
    murderers—Pennsylvania—Case studies. | Female
    offenders—Pennsylvania—Case studies. | Crime—Pennsylvania—Case
    studies.
Classification: LCC HV6533.P4 H663 2021 (print) | LCC HV6533.P4 (ebook) |
    DDC 364.152/308209748—dc23
LC record available at https://lccn.loc.gov/2021032087
LC ebook record available at https://lccn.loc.gov/2021032088

♾ The paper used in this publication meets the minimum requirements of American National Standard for Information Sciences—Permanence of Paper for Printed Library Materials, ANSI/NISO Z39.48-1992

CONTENTS

ACKNOWLEDGMENTS

Normally I would spend a great deal of time listing and thanking the curators of the many research facilities I visited during the course of writing the book you now hold. *Pretty Evil Pennsylvania*, however, was written during a pandemic.

I began this project less than two months before COVID-19 reached our shores and finished it as the nation began rolling out vaccines to end it. All of the Pennsylvania libraries, archives, and courthouses I usually rely on were closed for most (or all) of the time I spent writing. I was able to visit the Pennsylvania State Police Historical, Educational and Memorial Center before things turned truly dire. As always, historian Thomas Memmi opened the facility's invaluable collections and let me read everything they'd gathered on Irene Schroeder. Likewise, Lawrence County Commissioner Dan Vogler generously shared details of his ongoing efforts to keep alive the memory of Irene's victim, Corporal Brady Paul. Alcuin Books in Scottsdale, Arizona, answered my out-of-the-blue request to use a rare photo of Irene and her accomplices that was included among its inventory. These tasks were all accomplished in the first weeks of the creation of this manuscript.

And then . . . the world simply stopped.

The remaining chapters of this book are drawn from primary resources I managed to scratch out of online databases, tidbits I clawed out of historical newspapers, and details I dug out of the digital collections of libraries and archives. Still, to the dedicated vendors, organizations, and government offices that provided these hard-mined nuggets of gold, I offer great and sincere thanks.

Finally, I'd like to thank you—whatever your name, whatever your occupation—for your interest in historical true crime. You keep me going, literally and figuratively. Until (and after) our lives return to normal, be well, be happy, and be kind.

INTRODUCTION

The Girl.

Coined by notorious twentieth-century anarchist Alexander Berkman, this appellation (as he defined it) captures the quintessential, lawless female.

The Girl is valiant, intelligent, and capable of defending herself. She is a trusted comrade. Freedom—even life itself—are fair prices to pay if she is forced to choose between capture or disloyalty. The Girl always wins.

She is also a myth.

Sympathy is a fickle emotion. Judging by the women in this book, it can manifest for the most premeditated of criminals or dissipate in the wake of one unfounded rumor. Perhaps Berkman's idealized Girl could escape the consequences of her actions, praised and unscathed. For the women about whom you will shortly read, real life was less rhapsodic.

The more salacious the accused's theoretical motives, the larger the headlines and more plentiful the coverage. Editors enjoying the good fortune of reporting on a young and attractive criminal devoted a substantial expanse of copy to descriptions of her face, hair, body shape, and apparel. When the criminal was less comely, attention shifted to actions demonstrating her conniving nature or cold personality.

There is little doubt that the women detailed herein were guilty of the charges filed against them. Also clear is the fact that—unlike their male counterparts—public sentiment was heavily influenced by how far these women had strayed from the perceived "normal" feminine behavior of their day.

All of these crimes occurred in Pennsylvania and spanned the decades from the 1850s to the 1930s. They include horse stealing, kidnapping, financial fraud, aiding and abetting, murder, and, in one instance, possible "serial" murder far before that term entered the criminal lexicon. The goal is not to justify wrongdoing or rail against the punishment. Rather, the goal is to delve below the shallow surface of these transgressions and reach a deeper truth: that the details of these crimes were preserved, in large part, simply because their perpetrators were women.

Esther Sollenberger Good serves as the perfect first case study. In June 1895, when neighbors in Bowmansville, Lancaster County, first heard that the respected sixty-one-year-old matriarch was on her deathbed, they were shocked and saddened. "Hettie," as she was known, was an exemplary member of her community: a good wife, mother of four, and practicing Mennonite. Friends came by the dozen to visit one last time, knowing that the consumption that racked her weakened body would soon steal her soul. When Hettie insisted that Reverend Benjamin Horning be called to her bedside, no one was surprised. She was, after all, a good, God-fearing woman. What Hettie confessed to the good reverend and several additional witnesses, however, would stun not only the village but most of Eastern Pennsylvania, where the story quickly spread. Hettie wasn't the woman everyone believed her to be. Many said they *knew* something was wrong with her all along. And, if the whispered rumors of depravity were true, she was the worst kind of murderess: one who—forty years earlier—viciously murdered her newborn, poisoned her grandmother, and very probably killed her own mother.

Philadelphia's Mary Ridey was described by one jailhouse visitor as "perhaps the handsomest woman ever convicted in this city or any other." Mary had gone to a bar in fierce pursuit of her husband, John. She ended up inflicting mortal stab wounds on two brothers—Isaac and Joseph Sides—who attempted to intervene. Mary told the judge she'd never had the love of a mother, which left her bereft of knowledge of the difference between virtue and crime. Upon her pardon by Governor John W. Geary, those opposed to his leniency averred that the reason for such a miscarriage of justice could only be that Mary, through her purported house of ill-repute, had dirt on him and other politicians. But, if that is the case, why did she go to trial at all?

Salome Whitman was a twentieth-century "bad girl"; she was the first woman convicted of stealing horses in the Commonwealth of Pennsylvania. The twenty-year-old was described by one court observer as "pretty and muscular." Her daring deeds captivated newspaper writers. They were, however, wasted on the jury, who never bought the argument that she was coerced by career criminal and gang leader Abe Buzzard. When news spread that Salome became pregnant during her time in prison, it was proof to many that her reputation as a vixen manipulator was well-earned.

Emma Bickel painted herself as a woman used, abused, and deceived. She admitted to shooting and killing William J. Menow but claimed it was because he fabricated their marriage certificate. For three and a half years, she believed herself to be his lawful wife. When the facts of his deception came to light, she waited inside a shuttered window for his approach and shot him through the heart. It was an amazing feat for a woman who said she'd never fired a pistol before that morning. The jury bought her defense of insanity. Emma's real problems began when she tried to prove her sanity was restored.

When news broke that John Wanamaker and other prominent Philadelphia businessmen and firms were the victims of fraud, no one suspected that the fiend might be a woman. Julia Lippincott may have been an underappreciated criminal, but her trail of forgery and theft left many con men wondering why they hadn't devised her schemes themselves. By the time of her eventual capture, Julia had manufactured $35,000 in fake mortgages—a fantastic sum in 1890. Julia said she would have paid the money back, but she lost it in the stock market.

Katie Dietrich was nineteen years old when she married Peter Soffel Jr. She had no occupation. Her husband was a saloon keeper. An ambitious young man, Soffel soon took a clerk position in the Allegheny County government. In 1890, he was named deputy warden of the county jail. Peter was promoted to warden in 1900, a position he abruptly relinquished two years later. He couldn't very well stay on—especially since his own wife had helped two murderous brothers escape, one of whom was her lover.

The Mad Murderess. That is the nickname Bertha Beilstein earned after shooting her sleeping mother three times. Bertha—a wealthy Pittsburgh debutante—instantly regretted her actions and next attempted to dispatch herself. Amazingly, one bullet to the chest and another to the head failed to accomplish the mission. Instead, she was arrested and taken to an insane asylum from which she escaped seven years later. For months, police searched for Bertha, but even after her death, the story grew stranger.

Helen Boyle lived in a time when women still benefited from certain assumptions. That they're naturally maternal, for instance, and would never dream of hurting a child. It's what made Helen's headlong leap into a life of crime so discomforting. She and James S. "Lefty" Boyle's heartless kidnapping of nine-year-old Billy Whitla forced the public to reevaluate its stereotypes of the fairer gender.

The final stop on our tour of female notoriety is the first woman to be electrocuted in Pennsylvania: Irene Schroeder. She and her lover, Glenn Dague, operated their tag-team career as armed robbers using Irene's six-year-old son as a shield against suspicion. For weeks, they struck at will. In December 1929, the couple crossed paths with highway patrolman Corporal Brady Paul. The encounter left Paul dead and the public calling for Irene's execution.

You may view these stories differently because the perpetrators were women. That may even be justified. The fact is, though, that the one arena in which women have proven themselves undeniably equal to men is in the commission of crime.

1

HETTIE GOOD'S DEATHBED CONFESSION

On the 7th of June 1895 at Bowmansville, Lancaster
County, Pennsylvania, Sister Hettie Good, widow of
Jonathan Good, deceased, aged 61 years, 4 months and 19
days. Buried on the 10th in the Bowmansville graveyard.
She was a member of the Mennonite denomination for a
long time previous to her death. Four children survive her to
mourn over her departure. Funeral services by Henry Good
and Benjamin Horning, from 2 Cor. 5:10.

If you've ever wondered if the content of one's obituary matched the quality of her character, consider the case of Esther "Hettie" Sollenberger Good, who lived in the small Lancaster County village called Bowmansville in Brecknock Township in the nineteenth century. Anyone reading this abbreviated version of her life would assume Hettie to be a God-fearing, beloved, and respected widow—and she was . . . right up until her burial. That is when the rumor dam broke and the story of Hettie's bizarre deathbed confessions poured forth, like wine at the last supper.

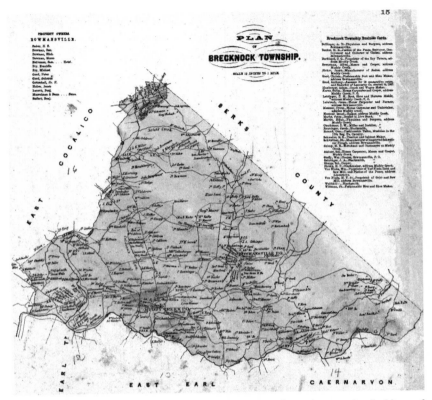

This 1864 map of Brecknock Township, Lancaster County, shows the many landholdings of the Good family and their proximity to the village of Bowmansville.

Sister Hettie, the pious farmer's wife, was—by her own admission—a murderess. She had taken two lives, and with hindsight as their best investigative tool, neighbors surmised there might have been one additional victim she hadn't acknowledged.

Like Quakers, the Mennonites found a harbor from persecution in William Penn's colony, first arriving in the early eighteenth century. Bowmansville was (and still is) a Mennonite stronghold. The church Hettie Good faithfully attended was likely founded by one of her husband's ancestors.

Hettie's own family situation is somewhat unclear. Her mother, Anna Hutchison Sollenberger, was twenty-two when Hettie was born, yet Hettie, in her late teen years, lived with her grandparents, David and Esther Hutchison. As a girl, Hettie enjoyed the attention of a number of suitors. She was particularly taken with young William Griffiths of neighboring Berks County. The couple quickly became inseparable, so it was no surprise when they announced they would be married. Supposedly, though, Hettie's grandparents strongly disapproved of this union. It was this resistance that Hettie used as an excuse to break off the engagement with the bewildered Griffiths.

Shortly after the split from Griffiths, Hettie met Jonathan G. Good. When Jonathan was just three, his father died, but Jonathan and his brother remained extremely close to their paternal grandfather, Joseph Good. When Joseph died, the substantial landholdings of the Good family passed to Jonathan, providing him with a reliably comfortable life.

Jonathan likely knew no more of Hettie's relationship with Griffiths than anyone else outside her immediate family, likely one reason they wed early into the courtship. Hettie was barely twenty years old and soon a mother. The Goods' first daughter, Amanda, preceded three more children, born over the next decade. To all outward appearances, Hettie lived as most farmers' wives did in that region of the Commonwealth. She tended her kitchen garden, cooked, cleaned, laundered the family's plain clothes, and reared the children. Indeed, the Goods seemed like a fine and close family. Still, there were quiet rumblings about Hettie's temper. More than one person witnessed Hettie's raucous verbal brawls with her younger brother, John, who had taken up residence on their grandparents' farm. The homestead seemed a near-constant source of strife between the siblings, but there was nothing to suggest that Hettie was dangerous—merely cantankerous.

In the summer of 1883, forty-eight-year-old Jonathan Good fell ill. He was running a fever. Pain radiated through his abdomen. He became too fatigued to rise from bed, let alone work the farm. On August 10, he succumbed to typhoid fever. Hettie was suddenly responsible for the welfare of four children and the management of the family's considerable farmland.

As the years passed, the widow seemed to grow sullen, angry, and depressed. Some friends and neighbors assumed the changes were byproducts of the loneliness brought on by the loss of a spouse. Others, however,

This image shows Esther "Hettie" Good's signature on the affidavit of the death of her husband, Jonathan G. Good. Jonathan died before learning of Hettie's murders.

suspected that something much darker was at play. On Monday, June 3, 1895, these more skeptical observers were proven correct.

While the family housekeeper, Katharine Steffy, was busy elsewhere in the home, Hettie made her way to the kitchen. There she found a long, sharp butcher knife and drew it several times across her throat. The horrific wound was nearly five inches long. It was too far up her neck to be fatal, but one of the slices nicked her windpipe. Hettie was already suffering from consumption (tuberculosis). The leaking windpipe made her breathing even more labored and painful.

Somehow, after self-inflicting the gruesome wound, Hettie made it back to her bed where she presumably laid down, in anticipation of death. That is where Katharine found her, resting atop a mattress saturated with her own blood.

The family summoned Dr. John Long, who decided not to stitch the wound the day it occurred but rather a day after the suicide attempt. He apparently assumed that—between the blood loss and the consumption— Hettie's death was imminent. He was wrong.

Late in the evening on June 3, Hettie made a strange request. She wanted William Griffiths brought to her bedside. No one knew why, but she would not rest until her old lover was brought from nearby Mohnsville, Berks County, to the Good farm in Bowmansville. It took some convincing to make Griffiths leave his own home and family to make the trip, but with his wife's blessing (probably borne out of unbridled curiosity), he made the journey.

William Griffiths arrived at Hettie's house just before midnight. There was no way he could have truly steeled himself for the scene that awaited him, even if he had been warned of her condition. Hettie's throat was bandaged. Air involuntarily escaped her body, making her speaking voice grotesque and unrecognizable. And the true horror had not yet begun. Hettie had a confession to make. It was one that poor Griffiths could never unlearn.

Their breakup, Hettie explained, was not simply a product of her grandparents' disapproval of their union. Hettie had, in fact, ended the relationship, she told Griffiths, because she was pregnant. Wanting to keep the baby a secret, she called off the marriage before her predicament became obvious.

For a brief few moments, Griffiths must have believed he was about to learn of a son or daughter whose existence had been a secret to him. But Hettie's story had no such surprise ending. She did have a baby, she told him: a normal, healthy infant. Yet, after its birth, Hettie made a terrible decision: she wanted the baby gone, and the only way to do that was to kill it. At three days of age, Hettie shoved her finger down the newborn's throat, hoping to suffocate it. To her fury, it did not work. So, she took a far more expeditious and violent route. She carried the baby outside and thrashed it against the mountain stone walls of her grandparents' home until its life was extinguished. Afterward, she buried the little body in the garden and never spoke of it again.

If Hettie viewed this confession as a cathartic unburdening, William Griffiths—the man she once professed to love—must have seen it as a life sentence. For the rest of his days, these abominable images of the murder of his daughter must surely have haunted his idle thoughts and darkest dreams. In sharing the atrocity, though, Hettie hoped she would be absolved of the brutal infanticide. More amazing, Griffiths was just the first to hear Hettie's tale of murder.

On June 4, when it appeared Hettie was not yet prepared to give up her troubled ghost, Dr. Long stitched the wounds on her neck. This procedure complete, Hettie next called the Reverend Benjamin Horning to her room. In a fiendish instant replay, she again described the slaying of her infant child. It was almost as if she was playing to the audience of friends and family members that had gathered around her bed because she now moved on to the next chapter of her confession.

For some years, Hettie had cared for her elderly grandmother, Esther Hutchison. Bedridden and needy, the old woman was a constant source of work and worry. Whether instigated by her grandfather, David, or whether the seed germinated inside Hettie, no one can say. Either way, the pair decided it was time for Esther's suffering (and theirs too, apparently) to end. Either by an overdose of medicine or a large serving of poison, Hettie killed the grandmother who had raised her.

Confessions concluded, Hettie's silent audience waited as she struggled to deliver one final pronouncement: "I am lost, and I will go to hell."

Reverend Horning comforted Hettie as best he could and returned on Wednesday to convince her to repent her deeds rather than just relive them. Hettie, though, was convinced this was useless. The memory of her evil actions continued to torment her. As soon as the reverend left her home, Hettie went once again in search of the large butcher knife that had failed her the first time. Not finding it, she considered other methods of suicide. A neighbor, Mary Bowman, passed by the house and noticed, through the window, Hettie testing the strength of a torn strip of calico fabric as if considering it for a noose. At this point, the family decided that Hettie could never again be left alone.

On Friday, June 7, 1895, Hettie Good's death wish was finally granted. She drew her last breath in bed and was buried three days later in her plain clothes, in a plain coffin. A large coterie of mourners attended the funeral and burial, but most came to assuage their curiosity rather than pay their respects. Word of Hettie's confessions had spread like feathers in the wind, and these morbid tourists had come to witness the final chapter in this bizarrely disturbing story. But Hettie was not quite finished revealing her secrets.

Just when people around Lancaster County thought they knew all of Hettie's sins, they were left to consider one final transgression. Several years previously, Hettie's mother—much like her grandmother—had deteriorated to the point of requiring near-constant care. Hettie, hoping to hand off the burden of these ministrations, demanded that her brother take their mother into his home on the former Hutchison farm. John declined, saying he'd previously proposed doing just that, only to be met with Hettie's refusal. This disagreement was apparently the root of the riotous arguments and permanent hard feelings for which the siblings were known.

When Hettie's mother died, the villagers found it a bit surprising as there seemed to be no specific, precipitating cause. After hearing Hettie's history of violence, though, speculation ran rampant. Did Hettie hasten her mother's death as she had her infant child and her aged grandmother? The coincidence was too strong to ignore. True or not, the people of Bowmansville concluded that Hettie's victims numbered three, not the two she'd admitted to killing.

In time, the infamy of Hettie's confessions receded into the memories of the town elders. Even nearly 130 years after her death, no one wants to discuss the lives wrecked by her need to share her tales of murder. Instead, the people of faith with whom she lived and whose ancestors remain in Bowmansville today likely take heed of Reverend Horning's funeral sermon. Quoting 2 Corinthians 5:10, he said, "For we must all appear before the judgment seat of Christ, so that each of us may receive what is due us for the things done while in the body, whether good or bad."

In the case of Hettie Sollenberger Good, those things were very bad indeed.

2

MURDERESS MARY RIDEY AND THE QUESTIONABLE PARDON

Prostitution wasn't born in Philadelphia, but it was certainly fed, nurtured, and grown there. In the City of Brotherly Love, founded by pious Quakers, the oldest profession was so prevalent that an anonymous writer in 1849 published a directory of brothels, complete with ratings and recommendations. This directory's creator estimated that there were 10,000 prostitutes working at that time, although those were just the ones who plied the trade publicly. Considering the city's population was 350,000, that was one sex worker to every thirty-five residents. The true number of prostitutes, however, was likely significantly higher.

There was a brothel for every budget in Philadelphia in the mid-nineteenth century. Some madams were renowned for the quality of both their houses and their whores, who, before the main act, would entertain men with singing or piano playing. The best houses guaranteed cleanliness, privacy, and security—a dominant concern for the public figures and married men (and women) who frequented them. These high-end establishments were known as temples of pleasure; they were first-class bed houses and houses of assignation.

The counterparts to the "classy" call girls were described in far less charitable terms. While the expensive brothels were the haunt of "gentlemen," these were the haven of the "common people." It was as though buying the company of a high-priced companion was a badge of honor. The pitiful creatures charging only pennies for their bodies and souls, however, were somehow more reprehensible—more sinful—than their more elegant sisters in the trade. After all, who would choose an "ugly, vulgar, and drunken" prostitute when you could spend the evening in comfort with a young lady "fresh from the country and perfectly safe."

Mary Ridey was many things. Fresh from the country she was not.

Mary operated her house of ill repute during the Civil War, a time when the city was booming both economically and in population. Philadelphia was the Union Army's largest supplier of weapons, uniforms, and men. Nearly three-quarters of the male population went to war for the North. Tens of thousands of men from nearby states passed through Philadelphia on their way south—a vast potential clientele for the busy brothels.

Mary's establishment was not listed in the city directory of brothels, so there's no way to know how it might have been rated. Located less than a mile from the waterfront, however, it was a convenient stop for the thousands of laborers and passengers who passed through Philadelphia's ports.

Mary was married to John Ridey. While Mary operated her bar-slash-whorehouse, John operated a separate dram shop, a tavern that sold liquor in smaller, restricted quantities. Like the rest of the nation, most Philadelphians were still processing the bloody aftermath of the war between the states and the assassination of President Abraham Lincoln, which had occurred only three months previously. None of these weighty thoughts seemed to enter the consciousness of Mary and John, though. They were obsessed with their own petty disagreements. The couple's fights were loud and often violent. It wasn't unusual for John to go off for days and not tell Mary where he was. An enraged and often intoxicated Mary would track him down, hellbent on punishment. Such was the case on July 3, 1865.

Mary's bartender and bodyguard, Ferdinand Albert, arrived at the house that day to find John and Mary in their predictable state of rage. Mary

A
GUIDE TO THE STRANGER,

OR

POCKET COMPANION

FOR

THE FANCY,

CONTAINING

A LIST OF THE GAY HOUSES

AND

LADIES OF PLEASURE

IN THE CITY OF BROTHERLY LOVE AND SISTERLY AFFECTION.

PHILADELPHIA: 1849

This directory of Philadelphia brothels predated Mary Ridey's establishment but illustrates the abundance of prostitutes in the City of Brotherly Love.

stormed off to her sister's house, taking Albert with her. She eventually decided to go back home, and Albert went his own way on an errand.

Mary's boarder, Margaret Reeves, accompanied Mary to her bedroom. She watched as Mary took off her dress, retrieved a dagger from under her pillow, and tied it around her waist. Mary then changed into a dark blue dress. She then pulled a small billy club from under her bed, slipped it into her dress pocket, and left.

All morning Mary had complained of a stomachache. Mary's go-to restorative for digestive ailments was a concoction of brandy and pepper, known in previous centuries as a cure for everything from cramps to malaria to molting chickens. She stopped for four separate doses at various establishments on her way to meet Ferdinand Albert at Third and Brown Streets near the home of brothers Joseph and Isaac Sides. Her inevitable drunkenness made her approach to the Sideses' home anything but stealthy. Mary was convinced John Ridey was hiding from her there. She was right, but he'd slipped out the back door when he heard her coming.

As Albert waited out front, Mary charged inside and screamed for John to reveal himself. Twenty-four-year-old Joseph Sides, who was in a back room that served as a tavern, told Mary that John had already left. Enraged and intoxicated, Mary ran up to Joseph. "Then you'll do!" she shouted as she pulled the knife from under her dress. With surprising speed and savagery, she plunged the blade into Joseph's chest and stomach, again and again.

Seventeen-year-old Isaac Sides heard Mary's words and his brother's cries of pain, but he hadn't seen the attack. It was only when Joseph said, "She's stabbed me," that Isaac understood the horror of the situation. Mary tried to flee through the front door, but the sickly, one-hundred-pound Isaac gripped her by the hair and shoulders. Mary flung around to face him and, as she did, sank the blade of her dagger deep into his abdomen.

Incredibly, neither of the brothers yet realized that the wounds Mary had inflicted were mortal. Both ran after her, as did Albert. William Daily, one of the Sideses' tavern customers, also gave chase. Mary was fast, but he was faster, and he even passed Albert, who was directly behind her.

Albert shouted a warning to Daily: "If you stop her, I'll shoot you."

Daily gave up the pursuit.

Mary Ridey returned home, where she quickly removed the blood-soaked blue dress. Boarder Margaret Reeves asked her what happened. "I've killed Joe Sides," Mary replied. She then bathed, re-dressed in a man's sailor suit and Albert's Kossuth hat, smeared ash on her upper lip, and slipped out the back door onto Noble Street. Unfortunately for Mary, however, her frenzied attack, wild screams, and dramatic chase scene drew the attention of countless witnesses. Within seconds, she was seized by the police and led to jail. She was right about Joseph; he was already dead. His brother Isaac would die the next day, and Mary would face two counts of murder.

The trial didn't start until November. Mary secured the services of three attorneys, including the eminent German lawyer Frederick Dittman. Perhaps he was attracted to the case because Mary, too, was of German heritage. Dittman's co-counsel, Lewis C. Cassidy, would years later become Pennsylvania's attorney general. David Paul Brown rounded out the trio. In addition to working as a lawyer, Brown was also a noted poet and playwright well-known for his fierce anti-slavery views. Together, the three men were the nineteenth-century version of O. J. Simpson's twentieth-century legal "dream team." But the prosecution also had a star. Assistant District Attorney Thomas Bradford Dwight was the son of attorney William T. Dwight, a respected Philadelphia attorney turned clergyman. His grandfather, the well-known Timothy Dwight, was a former president of Yale University. His moral center could not have been more distant from the woman he sought to jail.

By noon on the first day of the trial, all of the prospective jurors had been exhausted, with only five seated. The sheriff was ordered to bring his jury wheel into the courtroom. Used as late as 2014 in at least one Pennsylvania county, the "wheel" was actually a tin barrel into which jurors' names were dropped. After a few rotations of its handle, the names were thoroughly mixed and randomly drawn. In Mary's trial, 250 names were deposited into the wheel, and from them, fifty men were selected as potential special jurors. By late afternoon, this effort finally yielded twelve seated jurors, and proceedings resumed.

In order to convict Mary of murder, the state needed to prove two elements: motive and intent. From the start, Dittman argued that prosecutors had failed to do so.

At the time of Mary's trial, Pennsylvania was one of the first states to recognize two degrees—first and second—of murder. Specifically, the controlling statute read:

> All murder, which shall be perpetrated by means of poison, or by laying in wait, or by any other kind of willful, deliberate and premeditated killing, or which shall be committed in the perpetration or attempt to perpetrate any arson, rape, robbery, or burglary, shall be deemed murder in the first degree; and all other kinds of murder shall be murder in the second-degree.

The key to winning a first-degree murder case was proving that the defendant understood that his or her actions (i.e., intent) would result in the death of another human being. It was the element of intent that, according to Dittman, the Commonwealth lacked in its case against Mary Ridey.

Dittman told the judge and jury that Mary did not enter the Sideses' premises with the clear intent to kill, but rather she was in a state of homicidal mania—what we would today call temporary insanity. Should the jury not buy that defense, Dittman attempted to slip in alternatives. During one round of questions, he stated that Mary's mother had first prostituted her at the age of thirteen. The prosecution, quite rightly, objected to Dittman's offer of facts not in evidence, and the judge ordered the testimony stricken from the record. This didn't stop the wily attorney from introducing yet another option: that Mary's mother's criminal behavior passed genetically to Mary, creating a condition that Dittman described as "moral insanity." Mary's lack of early supervision and care changed her from a mild, peaceable child to a woman tainted by the bad company she kept. And, if these sympathetic theories weren't enough for the jury to chew on, Dittman threw them one final bone: Mary was far too intoxicated to understand what she was doing the day she took two lives. She, therefore, lacked any ability to form intent.

Mary was first tried for killing Joseph Sides, the older of the two brothers. It took just two days for both sides to present their evidence. On December

1, 1865, the jury found her guilty of second-degree murder, a verdict that took execution off the table.

The trial for the murder of Isaac Sides began on January 3, 1866. Initially, Mary's attorneys planned to fight the charge by repeating the strategies used in her first case. In the end, she pleaded guilty to second-degree murder, a move that simply expedited the inevitable. Twenty-something Mary Ridey would serve eighteen years and six months in the penitentiary, a sentence the judge believed fairly balanced her crimes against her young age.

Public opinion was split on the result. More tenderhearted Philadelphians believed Mary's hard life led her to make outrageously poor—and, in this case, deadly—decisions. Her entire life had been spent in brothels, her own mother forced her into prostitution, and she was an alcoholic from a shockingly young age. The eighteen-year sentence seemed to these observers extreme and without benefit to Mary or society at large. Also not lost on her supporters was the fact that she was young and easy on the eyes. In one newspaper story written months after her sentencing, a reporter described the murderess as "the most beautiful woman ever convicted in this or any other city." He noted that her "unkempt hair fell in massive waves to her waist." He assured his readers that Mary regretted her actions, something he knew was true when he stared into her "ebony eyes." All efforts would be made, this writer assured, to see that the newly elected Governor John W. Geary would sign a speedy pardon.

People with more conservative opinions felt that serving nearly two decades behind bars was a gift and that Mary should have been hanged. Even one of the district attorneys decried the leniency of her sentence. If every harlot could use a knife to avenge her perceived slights, many wondered, how soon would it be until lawlessness overtook the city? Some even went so far as to suggest that if juries continued to allow criminals back on the streets, the citizens' only recourse might be a Vigilance Committee that meted out its own punishment.

For her part, Mary served her sentence compliantly. The conspiratorially minded believed her calm resolve resulted from her knowledge of compromising information. Even Governor Geary was susceptible, they claimed, although if he was, he took his time in responding to her threats. But common sense didn't stop the rumor mill. Why was Mary's pardon Geary's last official act before leaving office? Why was no official explanation supplied for Mary's pardon? Surely, Geary or his cronies were clients of Mary's. Why else would she receive such "special" treatment?

As with most conspiracy theories, the truth is usually far more mundane than the conjecture. Mary's pardon was actually the result of the efforts of her aging father, who doggedly worked for her release. In the end, it was determined that—based on Mary's sad life story and previous alcohol dependency—the eight years she'd served were sufficient punishment.

Although Mary herself made no headlines after her release, her story was revisited again and again on anniversaries of the event. Over the decades, she became more of a "whore with a heart of gold" heroine than the enraged and intoxicated woman who killed Joseph and Isaac Sides. The story even evolved into one of self-defense: Mary protecting herself against two men trying to debauch her. In both versions, though, it is Governor Geary's motives that remain suspect. After all, what politician would pardon a prostitute unless she knew his secrets?

By the turn of the twentieth century, the population of Philadelphia exceeded 600,000. When contacted by a researcher studying the history of prostitution, notoriously corrupt Mayor Richard Vaux offered what he professed to be an accurate tally of sex workers in his city: 475 public prostitutes, 105 kept mistresses, 130 brothels, fifty houses of assignation, and 580 abandoned women. There's no way to know if Mary Ridey was among these assuredly minimized and purposely misleading tallies. If she was, the once young and beautiful Mary would have been fifty-something and near the close of what one Philadelphia doctor described as a life of "misery, poverty, and degradation" ending under the combined influence of "syphilitic poisoning and alcoholic stimulation"—a sentence far worse than even her harshest judges might have recommended.

3

SALOME WHITMAN, HORSE THIEF AND TEMPTRESS

The Welsh Mountains, contrary to their grand moniker, are actually a range of hills on the southern border of Earl Township in Lancaster County. Named after early Welsh immigrants (who were soon replaced by German settlers), the area sits several hundred feet above sea level. The fertile soil and abundant spring water made it a perfect place to situate a homestead or farm. The thick forest made it a perfect place to hide—and that is what dozens of outlaws did throughout the early twentieth century.

The Welsh Mountains of Pennsylvania were unique in that both black and white outlaws roamed its hills, although the two bands of robbers kept their enterprises separate. Nonetheless, they lived, stole, and secreted themselves in relative peace in the hills for generations.

Warnings about the Welsh Mountain bandits date back to 1790 when the *Pennsylvania Gazette* ran a story about the area's Green Banditti, a family gang led by a black man named Tom Green. Although Tom was killed in a robbery, his family carried on for generations and were prime architects of the Welsh Mountain legend.

By the mid-nineteenth century, one particularly miscreant white family ruled the hills: the Abe Buzzard gang. Their crime spree began before the Civil War when Abe's father terrorized the township. After the patriarch was killed during the war, his widow was left to raise nine children alone, a task for which she had little interest. She remarried and left the children mainly to their own devices. None attended school. Abe, the oldest, resorted to robbing clotheslines and henhouses to sustain himself and his siblings. His exploits and criminal organization evolved, and by the time he reached his twenties, there was a standing reward issued for his capture: $5,000 dead or alive.

Abe was captured several times, but, unfortunately for Lancaster County, he'd developed quite a knack for escaping jails. In 1882, it looked like his luck had finally run out when both he and his brother Ike were sentenced to thirteen years. Kismet once again smiled on the thief, and he was released early, only to announce a new career as an evangelist. Unsurprisingly, it didn't last. Abe Buzzard was soon back to stealing and hiding and running the largest criminal gang in the Welsh Mountains. Everyone knew who he was, and they either wanted to avoid him or emulate him. Even young girls knew his legend, though there was little chance that they could join Abe's bandit brigade . . . at least, that is, until Salome Whitman became the first woman from the mountain to birth her own folk tales.

Saturday, July 12, 1884, was a typical summer day in Pennsylvania. The strong storms that bruised the area created a good deal of damage and flooding but did little to break the humid, oppressive heat. Casper Showalter was accustomed to the uncomfortable weather and took his horse-drawn wagon out into the only slightly cooler evening air to visit a friend. He tied his team of horses outside his friend's house and thought nothing more of them. His nonchalance proved perilous moments later when he heard his wagon race away into the night. He would have undoubtedly laughed had anyone told him it was being driven by a woman.

Salome could not believe she got away with the theft. She drove to Martindale, then to Voganville, where her parents lived and where she fed the horses. From there, she traveled to New Holland and finally Blue Bell before turning up at the home of her grandfather, Christian Hess, the next day. She tried to sell the horses and wagon to Hess, but he wasn't buying.

If Salome thought she had made the trip unnoticed, she was wrong. Word quickly reached Showalter that his wagon could be found near the Hess home. There was little doubt in Showalter's mind that Abe Buzzard's

Salome Whitman's hard-living lifestyle eventually caught up to her. She died early, at age fifty-eight, of cirrhosis of the liver.

gang was responsible for the brazen theft, and he was half right. Salome stole the horses to impress Buzzard, perhaps even to win a place in his mob, but she wasn't an official conspirator. That didn't make her story any less sensational.

Salome Whitman was born in 1863. Her father, George Buck, worked as a laborer. Like most women of the day, her mother, Mary Hess, kept house and looked after Salome's younger siblings. Salome left home young and, at seventeen, took a position as a servant for another Earl Township family. At some point, she supposedly married a man named Abe Whitman, but no record of that union exists. Nonetheless, it was the story she told Constable William Sweigart when he arrested her three days later. She repeated the story to the justice of the peace who arraigned her. She even shared with a reporter the story that her husband was currently incarcerated in the Lancaster County jail. The journalist investigated the claim but found no such inmate.

Accuracy of her claims aside, Salome made for great ink. Newspapers across the state told the story of the first woman arrested in Lancaster County for horse theft. It was a "high crime" in the Commonwealth, one considered to be so notorious that the usual standards of proof were relaxed. A hundred years previously, she could have been executed for the crime. By the nineteenth century, however, stealing horses was no longer a capital offense, and Salome received a sentence of one year and eight months in the county jail.

Salome was housed with another female prisoner. As there was no separate wing for women, their cell adjoined one housing two men. The women's cell was once occupied by a scandalous convict by the name of Mary Wise—a shameless criminal who wasn't going to let incarceration spoil her fun. Mary had discovered that the wall between her cell and the next was merely a facade of loose plaster; a sort of mobile divider that could be removed or replaced at will. Whether Salome and her cellmate discovered this convenience themselves or if the men told them is not known. What is clear is that the foursome made recreational use of the opening. Almost immediately, rumors spread that there was something untoward going on in cell number 62. In this case, the rumors were right.

At the December 1884 monthly meeting of the prison board, after expelling reporters, the executive committee listened in horror to the lurid tales of Salome, her cellmate, and the two male prisoners next door. Apparently, the hole between the jail cells was only large enough for a thin person to utilize. Having gained a bit of weight while imprisoned, Salome remained in the women's cell while the thinner of the two men made regular visits. The arrangement worked for several weeks until someone witnessed the liaisons. And, as if the illicit visits weren't shocking enough, there was another badly concealed secret floating around: Salome was now pregnant.

Whether she was impregnated by one of the two male prisoners next door, arrived at the jail in this condition, or if she was even pregnant at all, we will never know for sure. One thing was obvious, though. By the time of Salome's release from jail in March 1886, she'd lost a substantial amount of weight. Unfortunately, she hadn't lost her propensity to make incredibly bad choices in men.

Salome exited prison on March 3 having served all twenty months of her sentence. Waiting for her in a carriage just outside the prison gate was Hen "Scaley" Smith, a notorious thief well-known to Lancaster County constables and jailers. Smith worked as a fence for the Welsh Mountain gang. He took the goods stolen in Lancaster and sold them in neighboring Berks County. Salome, apparently unconcerned about Scaley's felonious enterprise, announced to the crowd watching her departure that she and Scaley were soon to be married. Authorities had other plans, however, and two weeks later, Scaley was arrested for stealing chickens.

It seems Salome laid low for a few months after the arrest of her fiancé. In June, though, she was back to her old tricks and came before the magistrate on the charge of larceny. Clearly this situation was not to Salome's liking. During her hearing, she punched a witness against her in the face. Pandemonium broke out, and it took three officers to handcuff the wild young woman who, even while bound, attempted to escape on the way to jail.

Perhaps Salome experienced some sort of epiphany while in prison the second time. Or maybe she continued her life of crime but simply got better at evading arrest. Either way, by her mid-thirties, it appears that Salome had had enough of the bad life—or maybe she just recognized that the Welsh Mountains were changing. Once feared outlaws were slowly losing influence to far more powerful overlords: profit and religion. The Mennonite Church was the first to propose the idea that the best way to eliminate lawlessness in the region was to provide a legitimate means of earning a living. It opened a mission on the mountain to both provide work skills and employment. Shortly after that, a company called Silica Products capitalized on the vast revenues to be made from the sand and gravel hiding under the mountain soil. Horse and chicken thieves like Abe Buzzard, Scaley Smith—and, yes, even young, pretty Salome Whitman—were no match for corporations.

On April 30, 1896, now in her thirties, Salome married Harry Filson, an honest laborer, in nearby Chester County. The couple remained married for twenty-five years until Salome—Pennsylvania's first convicted woman horse thief—died of cirrhosis of the liver at age fifty-eight years, six months, and eleven days. But somewhere in the mountain, her legend lives on.

4

EMMA BICKEL
AND THE
INSANITY DEFENSE

To borrow an old cliche, Emma Bickel didn't marry well. To be fair, she wasn't given much of a head start in life. Her father was certifiably insane, she suffered from epilepsy (a condition several of her siblings shared), and she had little in the way of mentorship. Whether one or all of those reasons precipitated the murder of William J. Menow is difficult to ascertain, but we know, without question, that she killed him. We know this because she repeatedly, and quite voluntarily, confessed.

Philadelphia woke up to a cool and rainy day on September 3, 1883. When Emma Bickel left the Marshall Street home she shared with her parents and young son, she carried an umbrella. It was missing when she entered the home of Mrs. MaryAnn Horner at 1055 North Front Street. The two women knew one another (nearly all of the residents of the street knew Emma), but still, it must have been odd when Emma knocked on the door and asked MaryAnn's permission to sit in the parlor in the hope of seeing a friend pass by on the way to work. Nonetheless, MaryAnn complied and left Emma alone, partially concealed by the drapes, staring out the window onto the sidewalk. What the obliging neighbor did not know was that, in her pocket, Emma carried a .22-caliber, nickel-plated pistol. Five cartridges had been removed, leaving two for her use.

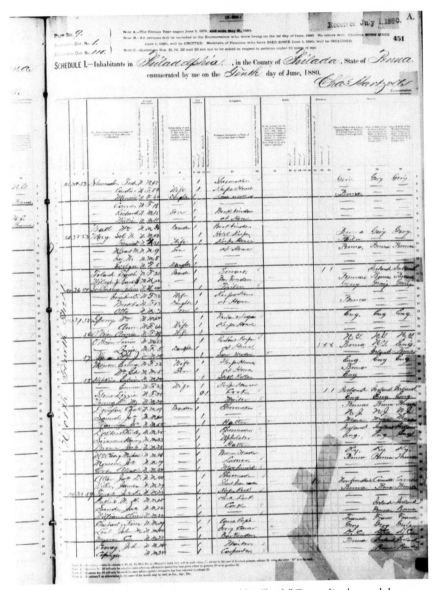

As this 1880 census shows, William J. Menow and his "bride" Emma lived several doors away from Emma's parents' North Fourth Street, Philadelphia home.

Within moments, Emma spotted twenty-eight-year-old William J. Menow and his namesake father making their way toward Disston Saw Works, where they both worked. Without hesitation, Emma drew the pistol from her purse. Her first shot went wild, but by the time she pulled the trigger a second time, she was locked on her target. The gun cracked, and the younger Menow reeled around, staggered several steps, then fell to the ground near the intersection of North Front and Poplar Streets.

Menow's co-worker, Henry Vokes, had been seated inside a nearby tavern when the first retort rang out. He thought nothing of it. When the second quickly followed, he ran outside to learn the circumstances. He saw Menow lying on the sidewalk and went to check his injuries. Within seconds, a young lady stood beside him. She gazed calmly down at the scene.

"He's been shot," Vokes announced.

"Yes," Emma agreed. "I'm the one who shot him."

As Vokes and the elder Menow carried William into a nearby cigar store, another bystander, John McLees, detained Emma. She assured McLees she would not try to flee and once again confessed to the shooting. A police officer patrolling nearby quickly arrived on the scene. The officer and McLees led Emma to the cigar shop where William Menow lay dying. When Menow expelled his last breath, the officer took Emma to the Tenth District Station to formally arrest her. From there, she was transported to Moyamensing Prison to await arraignment. As she quietly waited in her eight-foot-by-twelve-foot cell, stories of her suspect past and even more questionable present circulated.

"Did you hear?" the street gossips asked one another. "That woman, Emma Bickel, and the man she shot were living as husband and wife—but they were never married!"

"I heard she never divorced her first husband!" came the whispered response.

The truth of Emma's marital history, however, was far more complicated and salacious than even these tongue waggers could imagine.

Emma's life changed dramatically between 1870, when she was a thirteen-year-old child, and 1880, when she was a twice-married mother of a five-year-old son. The problem was, she wasn't quite sure if either marriage was legal.

Around the age of sixteen, Emma met Edward Bickel of Camden, New Jersey, the town located directly across the Delaware River from Philadelphia. The couple was married shortly thereafter, and, in 1875, they had a son they named William Edward Bickel. Whether Edward was always a violent man or if his outbursts started after marriage and fatherhood, we can't guess. He was, though, unrepentantly savage and, on several occasions, beat Emma so badly her face was nearly unrecognizable.

It took several years, but Emma finally reached her breaking point. She retained the services of a divorce attorney who, several weeks later, assured her she was unencumbered from Edward Bickel and free to seek new relationships. For whatever reason, the attorney lied. As it turned out, Emma and Edward were never really divorced. When she met William J. Menow several months later, Emma truly believed she was a single woman.

Menow and Emma were introduced by one of his co-workers. That man was smitten with Emma himself and was heartbroken to see the immediate attraction between his friend and would-be sweetheart. In front of Emma's mother, Menow behaved like the perfect suitor. He showered her daughter with attention, treated her grandson as his own, and referred to his mother-in-law by affectionate nicknames. Still, Ann Sperry felt a twinge of suspicion that was not at all quelled by Menow's constant waving of a copy of his and Emma's marriage notice, published in the October 15, 1878, issue of the *Public Ledger*. "Married on the 15th of October, 1878," it read, "by the Rev. J. B. Carter, William J. Menlow to Emily [sic], daughter of William Sperry of this city."

Emma and Menow rented a home on North Front Street, two doors down from the Sperry family. William's work as a saw maker was steady and respectable, for Disston Saw Works was the largest such manufacturer in the world. The union seemed to be a happy one. The couple was financially secure and supported by family. Ann Sperry soon learned, however, that her maternal radar had been right all along.

In March 1883, Emma filed a police report against Menow. It resulted in his arrest on charges of assault, battery, and desertion. In the hearing before the magistrate, Menow readily identified himself as Emma's husband. As to the criminal charges, the magistrate felt sufficiently convinced of the severity of the crime to set an $800 bail. Shortly after the couple left his chambers, the magistrate heard shouting and scuffling in the hallway. He ran to the scene to find Emma, pinned down by Menow and others, and holding a four-inch knife. Witnesses, including Menow, believed she was attempting to commit suicide. At some point, though, she became less intent on doing herself harm and more focused on him.

Emma dropped the charges against Menow. With legal recourse now off the table, she began stalking Menow in hopes of catching him alone. Several days before the murder, he spied her waiting outside the entrance to the saw works. Menow evaded her by leaving through the factory's rear entrance. Later that evening, Emma found him at a tavern. It wasn't hard to spot the large pistol in her small purse, and he seized it before she could use it. The next day, Emma went to a gun shop looking to borrow another pistol. She promised the shop owner she'd return it and, for collateral, left her umbrella and ring. It was this pistol she used to kill William J. Menow hours later.

By the time the coroner's jury convened, Menow's murder was all Philadelphia could talk about. A large crowd gathered to watch the proceedings and sat in fixed fascination as Lieutenant Beale of the Tenth Police District escorted Emma into the hearing. She wore a black silk dress with elaborate, braided trim. Her hands were bare, but she concealed her face with a dark purple veil. She sat at the defendant's table with attorney A. S. L. Shields and sobbed loudly throughout the proceedings. When asked her name, she replied, "Mrs. Emma Bickel."

Several witnesses recalled the events of the day, including Emma's spontaneous confessions. Dr. Cadwalader, the coroner's physician, offered details of the carnage Emma's bullet wreaked on Menow's body. It entered the left side of the chest of the five-foot-six-inch man, where it pierced the heart sac, causing Menow to bleed out inside his own carcass. After sawing his way into Menow's chest cavity, Cadwalader found a quart of blood. Unsurprisingly, the coroner's jury found the cause of Menow's death to be Emma Bickel.

For his viewing, the family dressed William J. Menow in a new black suit, not that anyone filing past his coffin could see it. The deceased was obscured by the dozens of floral bouquets placed around his body.

Menow's parents opened the doors to their home at 10 o'clock on the morning of September 6. They had not planned on making their son's service a public affair, but the crowd outside their home grew so large they felt that they had no choice. For the next four hours, hundreds of people—most total strangers—passed by the coffin. At 2 o'clock, the body was taken to a burial vault. Many of those who waited outside the home followed the procession.

Though these curiosity-seekers did not know it, the big story of the day was not Menow's funeral but rather his—and Edward Bickel's—marital status to Emma. Newspaper reporters had finally discovered that both men had lied. Emma was never divorced from Bickel—and she had never been legally married to Menow. Menow had apparently hired someone to perform a ceremony, but it was not a legal union.

Equally interesting was the new behavior Emma exhibited in prison. She shrieked incessantly and constantly called for the guards.

"I must be released," she screamed. "I don't belong in jail. I am insane!"

Fearing Emma might commit suicide, jailers implemented special precautions. Self-harm was not the only threat to Emma's safety, however. Some members of the public believed the wheels of justice to be spinning far too slowly. William Menow's brother made several public and menacing remarks, not the least of which was a promise to kill Emma the first time he saw her. While this claim was quite specific, he regularly made alarming threats against women he knew and was generally viewed as unstable. Emma was, in effect, imprisoned not only for her crimes but also for her own protection. The only person permitted to visit her was her mother, Ann Sperry.

On November 26, the grand jury returned a true bill of indictment for murder against Emma, and her court date was set for April 1884.

The trial of the Commonwealth versus Emma Bickel was held in what Philadelphians called their "new" courthouse, an imposing Georgian structure that had actually been completed in 1867. Still, it was newer than the original courthouse built in the early 1700s. Prisoners housed at

Moyamensing were transported by a streetcar that reached as far as 8th and Sansom Streets. From there, Emma and her police escort walked more than half a mile to the courthouse.

Emma always wore black to court, a color that complimented her raven hair and the intensely dark eyes that so often hid behind a veil. Ann sat near Emma, almost within reach.

On the first day of trial, it took three hours to empanel the jury, who immediately assumed their role as fact finders. The district attorney began by explaining that all murders involving "lying in wait" were indeed first-degree murders. Emma's actions were willful, deliberate, and premeditated, the prosecutor said, and therefore, she must be found guilty.

The defense, of course, had a wholly different view. "In the thirty homicide cases I've defended," A. S. L. Shields said, "I've never so believed in heart and soul in my client's guiltlessness. An unknown power controlled that woman. Her defense is insanity. It is a fair and proper defense in this case."

There were no surprises among the district attorney's witnesses, except for perhaps the very first one. As William J. Menow's mother made her way to the witness box, she and Emma exchanged obviously hostile glances. As might be expected, she told the story from her son's perspective, repeating the lies he'd fed her. Emma was angry because William had cast her aside, Mrs. Menow said. And her son was just as shocked as everyone else to learn that their marriage wasn't legal.

A parade of familiar faces followed, most of whom had either testified at the coroner's hearing or attended the arraignment. Dr. Cadwalader repeated his autopsy findings. Menow's father testified that the two had been walking to work when the shots rang out. He'd ducked after hearing the first one, but his son kept walking only to be subsequently felled by the second. MaryAnn Horner testified she ran to the parlor after hearing the shots and reenacted the conversation for the court.

"Someone is shot!" MaryAnn told Emma.

"I know," Emma replied. "I shot him."

Henry Vokes repeated his story about Emma confessing to the shooting as he checked Menow's wounds. Police officer Mulvey recounted that Emma admitted to knowing and shooting Menow, and that she took the revolver from her pocket and gave it to him.

It wasn't clear whether or not Emma heard any of this testimony. For most of the first day of trial, she rested her head on the railing of the dock, seemingly too exhausted to lift it. Occasionally, she was shaken awake and administered brandy to bolster her strength.

Overall, it was a strong first day for the prosecution, and the case against Emma seemed watertight. The next day, though, the defense presented testimony that turned what the jury thought they knew of Emma Bickel on its head.

Emma's lawyers began by introducing her biography to the jurors. A. S. L. Shields drew a bleak picture of the young woman's life, including the repeated beatings dealt by Edward Bickel. This was followed by the shocking story of the fake divorce that left Emma an unwitting bigamist—or at least she initially believed.

The wide-eyed jury next learned of Emma's bogus marriage to William J. Menlow and the lengths to which he'd gone to convince her and her family that they were lawfully wedded: the forged marriage certificate and the fraudulent notice in the newspaper. They also heard of Menow's physical abuse against Emma.

Shields allowed the jury to fully absorb this information before initiating a second and more complex element of the defense which began by calling Ann Sperry to the stand. When asked if there was a history of mental illness in the family, Ann relayed a litany of examples beginning with Emma's own behavior. Emma attempted to commit suicide six or eight times, according to her mother. She'd tried drowning herself, cutting her own throat, and self-administering an overdose of laudanum. Emma had even threatened to kill her own son. The behavior didn't surprise Ann, whose own relatives were found legally insane and committed to an asylum. Her husband, Emma's father, was also insane, Ann revealed. She ended her testimony with a firm declaration.

"I believe my daughter was insane the day of the shooting."

The defense called other witnesses to report Emma's delusional behavior, but these laypeople were just opening acts for renowned expert witness

Dr. Henry M. Dwight, a specialist in diseases of the mind. Asked about Emma's condition on the day of the shooting, Dr. Dwight replied, "She was not a responsible being."

"Sane or insane?" he was asked.

"Insane," the doctor replied.

The prosecution cross-examined Dr. Dwight, but the approach was confusing at best. "If a woman madly in love with a man and excessively angry at him, should trail him for months and then shoot him, would you think her insane?" the district attorney asked. It sounded more like a question the defense might ask.

"I should suspect so," Dr. Dwight answered.

"But if a woman had epilepsy, neuralgia of the bowels, and the hereditary taint of insanity, what would you think?"

Tired of repeating the same answer, the doctor stood fully erect in the witness box, clapped his hands to fully draw the prosecutor's attention and shouted, "She's insane!"

On the third day of trial, testimony concluded. The judge offered a clearly biased charge to the jury. After again explaining the concept of "lying in wait," he told them, "In this case, I can't see any less degree of murder than the first." The presumption of the law is sanity, he lectured the jurors. "Mrs. Bickel's duty is to prove she is *not* sane."

Judge Mitchell continued. "There is a distinction between anger and insanity. Use your common sense, experience, and judgment to distinguish between them." At 6 o'clock in the evening, he sent the twelve off to deliberate. Neither Judge Mitchell nor the prosecutors expected to wait long for a verdict.

At 8 p.m., the jurors were called back to the courtroom. "Have you reached a verdict yet?" the court clerk asked.

"We have not," said the foreman. Nor would they any time soon. The first ballot taken showed that only four jurors believed Emma to be guilty. In the second ballot, taken just after midnight, the number of jurors favoring conviction shrank to two. By dawn, the finding was eleven to one in favor of exoneration. Just before entering the courtroom, they reached unanimity.

On Friday, May 2, 1884, the jurors filed into the courtroom in one unbroken, single line. All in attendance noticed the sour looks on their faces, a seemingly bad omen for Emily Bickel.

"You have reached a verdict?" the court clerk asked a second time, to which the foreman responded affirmatively.

"Stand up and look upon the prisoner," the clerk barked at the jurors. "Prisoner," he instructed Emily, "stand up and look at the jury."

Emily peeled back her veil. Her face was white and tight, and she looked as though she might topple over.

"What say you?" the clerk asked the foreman.

Dozens of pairs of eyes and ears focused fiercely on the jury foreman. He nervously lifted the verdict slip to his face, took a deep breath, and then whispered the verdict in such a low voice that no one—not even those seated next to him—could decipher his words.

The court clerk snapped the sheet from his hands. After reading its contents silently to himself, he bellowed the verdict to the impatient audience.

"Not guilty by reason of insanity."

To the strict Judge Mitchell's consternation, a gasp of relief burst forth from the spectators. Emily pulled the veil back down over her eyes and sobbed. Moments later, someone placed her son in her lap, and she hugged and petted him as if seeing him for the first time.

At 11:15 a.m., Emily descended the courthouse stairs, a free woman. She ignored the reporters shouting her name and returned to Moyamensing to await transfer to the Norristown Insane Asylum. The jury foreman was not as reticent in the face of the press.

"I know," foreman Grancell said to the newspapermen, "the feeling about acquitting a prisoner on this ground. I have criticized such verdicts myself, but when we remember from what a weak-minded stock the woman sprang and considered that she had been through enough to overthrow even a robust intellect, we could not believe her otherwise but insane."

Assistant District Attorney F. A. Bregy was briefer and less charitable. "She is no more insane that I am, and she should have been convicted."

Emma Bickel spent nineteen more days in Moyamensing Prison before Judge Mitchell finally signed the order of transfer to the State Hospital for the Insane at Norristown in neighboring Montgomery County. Even then, Emma waited three more days to be transported to the new facility. On May 24, she left the Reading Railroad Station on the 2:25 train to Norristown. She wore her now trademark black veil and was accompanied by her sister, Annie O'Brien, on the two-mile journey. When the train stopped, Emma was initially confused. "I didn't think we'd get here so quickly," she told Annie.

Up until the arrival at the asylum, Emma had exhibited a stoic countenance. It cracked when she was led into D Section, Ward 4, of the hospital. A score of mentally ill patients surrounded her. Emma burst into tears and dropped limply onto the small cot, the only furniture in her cell. The only thing she could see of the outside was a sliver of blue sky through her tiny window. She could not bear the thought of remaining in this madhouse and told her attorneys as much. Just two months after declaring herself insane, Emma seemingly made a miraculous recovery. She demanded her lawyers win her release.

A. S. L. Shields was loath to make such a request of the court so soon. After all, his client had willingly and frequently admitted to shooting William J. Menow. Only Shields's passionate insanity defense saved her from the executioner. How could he now, just weeks later, argue that she was cured? But by the fall of 1884, the attorney could no longer resist his client's wishes. On November 1, Emma presented a petition for habeas corpus to the Philadelphia Court of Quarter Sessions. Included in the filing was a powerful exhibit: a letter from Dr. Alice Bennett, the supervisor of the hospital's women's department. "Emma Bickel is not of unsound mind," Dr. Bennett wrote. "She has been fully restored to mental sanity and no longer needs the remedial care of the hospital aforesaid or any other, and therefore I respectfully request the discharge of the said Emma Bickel from the custody of said hospital authorities."

Concurring with Dr. Bennett was her colleague Dr. Rebecca S. Hunt, assistant physician at the hospital. "Emma Bickel has completely recovered reason and is safe to be at large," stated Hunt.

As Emma's attorneys presented evidence to Judge Mitchell, startling news came to light that nearly scuttled their efforts. To the judge's surprise, he learned that Emma had left the facility on four occasions with Dr. Bennett's approval. Twice she was escorted by an officer of the institution, once she left with a friend, and on the final occasion her trip was completely unsupervised. The district attorney was outraged. "You are an accomplice!" he shouted at Dr. Bennett. "You've let a crazy murderess wander the streets!"

The stunned Dr. Bennett said she then and still believed she had the authority to make these decisions for Emma as she'd done for other patients many times. Judge Mitchell agreed that Dr. Bennett had exhibited no malice and indeed had the authority to make such determinations. He was not, however, as sympathetic to Emma's request for release. Instead, he ruled that he'd been presented with no actual evidence to prove that Emma was cured of her insanity and, therefore, dismissed the petition of habeas corpus. Coincidentally, Mitchell based his decision on a law passed that same year. Called the Lunacy Law of Pennsylvania, it prevented the discharge of patients found insane while committing criminal acts unless a judge was satisfied that such patients had received proper treatment and were cured.

Emma viewed the setback as temporary and, a month later, requested a second court hearing. On December 6, a chipper, chatty Emma arrived at the courthouse in a bright blue dress topped by a silk dolman, a cape-like coat with a wide panel in the rear to accommodate the dress bustle. She was accompanied by Dr. Bennett, and the two conversed happily as they waited to be called before the judge—who postponed the hearing.

Two weeks later, Emma returned a third time. Once again, her lawyers argued that she was mentally healthy and that it was unlawful for her to be held in an insane asylum well after her insanity ended. Once again, the judge postponed his ruling. These trips to the courthouse repeated themselves again and again until finally, on February 10, 1886, Emma Bickel was set free from the institution that had housed her for nearly two years. Where she went and what eventually became of her is lost to history, but her ability to successfully escape culpability for murder based on an insanity defense became a blueprint for other women of her time.

In 1891, Josie Mallison Smith stalked and killed her lover by shooting him in the head on the steps of Philadelphia's Powelton Avenue train station. She'd intended to shoot herself in the temple immediately thereafter, but bystanders wrestled the gun away. From the instant of her arrest, it was made clear that her defense team would claim insanity. Friends of the murderess highly recommended she retain the services of A. S. L. Shields. After all, they said, look what he'd done for Emma Bickel.

5

THE FORGER
JULIA LIPPINCOTT

When the brothers Wanamaker opened their first store in 1861, they featured a wide range of merchandise and a fresh perspective on the age-old retail industry. Employees were promised shorter workdays and payments—in cash—at the end of each shift. Merchandise in the shop had one set price, not wildly divergent prices based on the day or customer, and it was clearly marked on the affixed tag. Wanamaker's most enduring contribution to retailing, however, was that it instituted the first "return" policy. If a customer purchased an item, he or she could return it at any time, for any reason, no questions asked. This unparalleled level of service was the foundation upon which their city-block-sized, iconic department store—bound by Thirteenth, Chestnut, Juniper, and Market Streets—was built in downtown Philadelphia. It was also what enabled thief and forger Julia Lippincott, nearly thirty years later, to steal from the venerable institution at will.

Julia was, on her first few visits to the fifteen-acre department store, greeted warmly. In her matronly, monochrome garb, Julia never exuded wealth. Then again, it was not Julia's money the retailer courted but rather her hotelier husband Edwin's. So, when Julia asked to speak to John Wanamaker's manager, her request was met with immediate attention.

"I'm hoping you can do me a favor," Julia said. "I'm not as well-known at other stores in the city as I am here and I'm afraid they may be hesitant to take my personal check."

"How can I help?" asked the manager.

"I have here a check made out to John Wanamaker. Could you possibly exchange it for one made out in the same amount, written from the store's account? I'm certain your competitors won't question that," she added with a smile.

"Of course," the eager manager replied. "Give me one moment."

He hurried to the store's business office, congratulating himself for going well above and beyond for a customer, just like John Wanamaker would have wanted. He suspected he might even be rewarded for such elite service. His fine mood was dashed several days later when he learned that Julia's check was worthless and that he had lost his employer hundreds of dollars. Worse, the manager was now in the awkward position of asking Julia to give the money back.

To his great relief, Julia apologized for her mistake. She'd simply used the wrong bank account.

"I'll send you another check," Julia promised.

"All's well that ends well," he assured her.

But it didn't end well. In fact, it didn't end at all. The second check was also bad, as was the one meant to replace it. So, Julia proposed another solution: she presented a promissory note, signed by her husband Edwin, and made out for the amount of her debt. All Wanamaker's had to do was take the note to the bank and the store would be paid. There was but one small problem: Julia Lippincott's husband Edwin had never seen—nor signed—this document. Making matters worse, these notes were appearing all over Philadelphia and neighboring New Jersey.

Edwin Lippincott was born in Medford, New Jersey, on June 18, 1825, to Quaker parents Mary Stokes and Job Lippincott. Self-described farmers, the Lippincotts accrued valuable and sizable land holdings in Camden County, as well as both Burlington and Atlantic Counties. Opened in the 1880s, Edwin's most successful and prestigious property was Haddon House in Atlantic City. Pennsylvania politicians, businessmen, and well-to-do families traveled from all corners of the state to summer or weekend at the impressive oceanfront hotel positioned at the sea end of North Carolina Avenue. Once there, pampered guests enjoyed the most luxurious, modern conveniences:

A drawing of Julia Lippincott. What she lacked in physical charisma she more than made up for in her ability to deceive.

steam heat, an Otis elevator, speaking tubes, electric lights, a dance pavilion, and, of course, ocean views from nearly every corner. Room rates started at $3 per day. Weekly stays cost as much as $30, depending on your accommodations—more than $800 in today's money.

What guests could not find at Haddon House were alcoholic beverages. Writers of the day described the hotel as offering "little or no attempt at gayety." Its patrons were "sedate people fond of rest and quiet." All of this by way of saying, as a Quaker, Edwin Lippincott neither imbibed nor served booze.

Like other fine establishments of its time, Haddon House announced its visitors to the newspapers. It was a beneficial marketing ploy that spurred tremendous word-of-mouth publicity. Anyone wanting to keep up with the Joneses could simply check the social column to learn where they were vacationing. It was not uncommon for the hotel's guest register to include the signatures of such notables as bank presidents, elected officials, and the retired idly rich. If one were so inclined, Julia realized, all one really had to do to counterfeit those signatures was to borrow the register and practice.

Julia Cullinan's upbringing was far less charmed than Edwin's. She was born in Philadelphia to Irish parents, neither of whom lived long enough to see her mature. Julia's father died when she was seven. Her mother followed him to the grave six years later, at which time Julia was adopted by her Quaker aunt and uncle, Margaret and David Scattergood. The couple also adopted Julia's cousin Mary, and the two were raised as sisters.

David Scattergood's level of conservatism made Edwin's look positively reactionary. David's grandfather, Thomas Scattergood, was so puritanical in his religious beliefs that—while serving as warden of Philadelphia's Eastern State Penitentiary—he once filed an official complaint against a volunteering Quakeress for sharing with inmates a doctrine not fully duplicative of his own.

Margaret Scattergood, history would indicate, was far less strident than her husband. One of her hobbies was speculating in the stock market—an unsurprising avocation considering that Philadelphia's was the first stock exchange in the nation. Whether purposefully or through Julia's own initiative, this fascination passed to Margaret's niece. Julia, however, went about scratching her speculative itch in far less legal ways.

Julia Cullinan and Edwin Lippincott married on February 19, 1877. Edwin was fifty-two, a steady, established counterbalance to forty-one-year-old Julia's more insurgent nature. How Julia hid her early financial losses is one of the biggest mysteries of their marriage. When Edwin fell ill, Julia was left to run Haddon Hall almost single-handedly. With such resources and authority at her disposal, temptation took the upper hand.

Haddon House enjoyed reliably brisk trade through the summer of 1899, and Edwin had every reason to believe his prized real estate holding would see him comfortably through his remaining years. On the last business day of the season, as employees emptied and shuttered the hotel, Edwin's attorney, M. R. Sooy, visited Edwin's home to deliver shocking and devastating news. Edwin, Sooy explained, was being sued by nine plaintiffs, including the Philadelphia Trust Safe Deposit Insurance Company, the First National Bank of New Jersey, as well as several other businesses and individuals. They all claimed that Edwin has presented bad or falsified notes or checks and were demanding payment.

At first, Edwin assumed he was the victim of some unknown criminal trading on his identity and reputation. Sooy soon convinced him, however, that the culprit was much closer to home.

Edwin called Julia into the drawing room, where attorney Sooy presented her with a stack of bad checks and forged promissory notes. There was no denying what she had done. Julia confessed, sobs and tears punctuating her admission.

Whether to protect his wife or his reputation, Edwin paid the debts, depleting a great deal of his personal fortune in the process. Had he known these obligations were but a small part of Julia's indebtedness, he may well have made a different decision. On February 17, 1890, two days before their thirteenth wedding anniversary, newspapers revealed the full extent of her machinations. Edwin awoke to learn his wife was nothing more than a common thief. Worse, she had fled in the middle of the night, leaving him to bear the brunt of her larcenous hobbies.

While it is impossible to know when Julia's financial crimes began, one thing is certain: she spared no one, not even the woman who had raised her. In the 1860s, Margaret and David Scattergood moved from Philadelphia to Camden, New Jersey, its sister-city directly across the Delaware River. They were viewed by many as not distinct locations but rather one large metropolitan area connected by a short ferry ride. Camden businesses (and certain individuals) were even listed in Philadelphia city directories.

It was in Camden that David Scattergood died in 1867, leaving Margaret real estate investments and substantial personal assets. Margaret died nine years later. Her will stipulated that her estate, including those assets inherited from David, be divided equally between her nieces, Julia and Mary. The total inheritance for each was valued at roughly $30,000.

Before Mary could realize her share, however, Julia removed David's bonds and deeds from the safe deposit box in which Margaret stored them. Shortly thereafter—and for reasons unknown—Julia began her concentrated attack on Mary's personal assets.

In 1883, Julia secretly negotiated a $1,800 loan against Mary's Medford, New Jersey, home. Over the next several years, she added two more mortgages, in the amounts of $1,000 and $1,200. She also took out two personal loans against the home's equity in the amount of $300 each. Julia managed to pay these encumbrances through a series of schemes, including forged checks, bonds, and promissory notes. No one was exempted from her list of targets, not family, friends, hotel guests, employees, or even servants. In one instance, she even forged the name of a local magistrate. But she always returned to her favorite victim, Mary Haines.

In 1887, Julia took out three more mortgages on Mary's home: one for $14,413.68, another for $3,000, and the third for $1,500 made in the name of H. H. Quicksall. At the time, the home was valued at just $8,000, yet the United Security and Trust Company of Philadelphia approved $19,000 in mortgages. It was this enormous accumulation of debt that shifted Julia's thievery into high gear.

In addition to stores like Wanamaker's and Strawbridge & Clothier, Julia left scores of other unwitting victims through the Philadelphia/Camden area. By 1889, she desperately needed to repay her loans. Based on her

> ## EDWIN LIPPINCOTT BURIED.
>
> **MEDFORD, N. J., July 16.**—Edwin Lippincott, husband of Julia Lippincott, and the victim of the latter's forgeries, was buried this afternoon in the Friends' Acre, close by Medford Meeting House. Impressive addresses were made by eminent speakers. There were present hundreds of Mr. Lippincott's friends from Atlantic, Camden, and Burlington Counties. Mrs. Lippincott was not present, although many thought she would change her mind at the last and request the jail officials to permit her to attend the funeral.

The burial notice for Edwin Lippincott leaves no doubt as to whom his family blamed for his death.

presumed knowledge of the hotel industry, Philadelphia broker Josiah Hearing entered into a business partnership with her. Using Hearing's money to make the down payment, the pair secured a lease on the Lochiel Hotel on 8th Street. It was to be renovated and renamed the St. Cloud. When it came time to pitch in her share, though, Julia gave Hearing a forged and worthless note for $600.

Even if Julia had possessed the resources to invest in the St. Cloud, it was clear the project would never generate revenue quickly enough to dig her out of her hole. So, she moved on to a bolder, more time-tested venture: note shaving.

Practiced by both banks and individuals, note shaving is a simple and lucrative exercise. It relies on the requests of lenders to discount their principal owed; for instance, a reduction from a $10,000 loan at 6 percent interest to a $5,000 loan. The lender agrees to this reduced principal but hikes the interest rate to 12 percent, 30 percent, or sometimes several hundred percent. In effect, unless the borrower enjoys a windfall with which he can pay the debt in total, the loan lives forever—a situation benefitting only the lender.

Julia learned about note shaving from Charles B. Wigton, who rented a summer cabin a stone's throw from Haddon House. Wigton, the wayward son of a successful Philadelphia industrialist, was also the treasurer of Glamorgan Iron Company in Juniata County, Pennsylvania. Unfortunately, Wigton was also in debt and sought to rectify his finances by embezzling from his firm. Shortly after Julia's crimes came to light, Wigton was arrested and charged with stealing more than $100,000.

On February 19, 1890, the ailing Edwin Lippincott and destitute Mary Haines traveled to Philadelphia to meet with attorney F. F. Brightly. As they left Edwin's home, both he and Mary assured the reporters camped outside the front door that they had no idea where Julia was hiding.

Once in Philadelphia, Edwin received a torrent of even more distressing news. More individuals had come forward demanding their bogus promissory notes be made good, including tramway owner and millionaire A. J. Widener. It was also discovered that, through broker George H. North, Julia had bought heavily on the margins. In other words, Julia borrowed the money used to execute her stock transfers from the investment firm itself. And unbelievably, there was even worse news to come.

Several years prior, Julia had purchased a lot of land in Atlantic City with a $2,500 mortgage she'd taken out both in her husband's name and in the name of his brother-in-law, Isaac Stokes. Edwin hoped it would be the last of the financial body blows dealt by his wife. It was not. The most devastating sucker punch—the one Edwin never recovered from—involved his precious Haddon House. Without Edwin's knowledge or consent, Julia had mortgaged the hotel to the tune of $40,000. Little of the principal had been repaid, and the loan was in arrears. Edwin had no choice but to sell his oceanfront treasure. Doing so would cover Julia's debts and loan against the Haddon House. It would also whittle Edwin's once comfortable assets down to less than $3,000.

Meanwhile, Julia was still on the lam. During her absence, several detectives staked out Edwin's home in Medford, New Jersey, still suspecting he might be complicit in her disappearance. Others assumed she'd fled to Canada where she would remain, free from American jurisprudence. What these investigators never guessed was that Julia, while evading cops, creditors, and newspapermen, would retain the services of the Philadelphia law firm Arundel and Moon.

Nearly a month after Julia seemingly vanished from New Jersey, attorney R. O. Moon made public a letter from Julia asserting her innocence against all charges of fraud, forgery, and theft. Even so, she refused to divulge her whereabouts. Meanwhile, Edwin was buying ad space in Philadelphia and New Jersey newspapers cautioning retailers, banks, and businesses that he would not take financial responsibility for Julia's commitments.

On April 10, 1890, a judge dismissed the suit filed by the Second National Bank of Atlantic City against Mary Haines, Isaac Stokes, and Edwin Lippincott. The ruling stated that the defendants' signatures on the plaintiff's contracts were forgeries, and therefore, the loans were fraudulently obtained. A subsequent Atlantic City grand jury determined there were sufficient grounds to indict Julia for this fraud. Simultaneously, the county of Camden also returned ten true bills of forgery and fraud against her.

In an incredible display of audacity, Julia wrote Edwin several letters during her absence, asking him to send jewelry and other valuables. He neither aided his wife nor told the police where she was hiding. Thanks to the dogged efforts of one Camden detective named James Henry—who received a tip saying Julia was living in Baltimore—she was discovered and arrested on July 1, 1890, in the home of her sister. It was after 10 o'clock on that evening when Henry led the subdued, matronly woman through Philadelphia's Broad Street train station. There he was met by a second detective, James Tate of New Jersey, who joined the party for Julia's trip to Camden's Central Station.

Julia Lippincott was confined to her cell just before midnight. Ever the schemer, however, she'd found a way between capture and arrival in Philadelphia to get a message to R. O. Moon. Henry and Tate were shocked to find Moon waiting for her at the Camden County jail. The detectives sat at a nearby table as Moon and Julia chatted nonchalantly about her case. Reporters soon joined this odd little conference.

Dressed in a black hat and black-and-white gingham dress, Julia looked as if she hadn't a care in the world. Even learning that she faced seventeen indictments in New Jersey alone seemingly made no impact.

"I haven't been hiding from justice," Julia explained in response to reporters' questions about her disappearance. "I am a willing captive. When the officer found me, I was ready to return to Camden."

Attorney Moon echoed her confidence. "I don't know whether there are any charges of forgery that can be proven against her," he said.

There was, though, one person with firsthand knowledge of Julia's guilt and duplicitous nature, and for days, she'd been asking him to secure her bail. Edwin, however, refused—nor would he agree to visit her in jail. As days passed without a reply from her husband, Julia transformed from the happy-go-lucky prisoner she once pretended to be into to the despondent, forlorn captive she truly was. Her depression worsened when she learned that Edwin had fallen ill and that his family feared for his survival.

Within two weeks of entering jail, Julia's weight plummeted to barely one hundred pounds. Large, blue circles surrounded her brown eyes, and her face, rapidly aging, was thin and haggard. She complained about the prison food, in particular the bean soup served daily. Friends (many of whom she owed money) brought more palatable fare such as steamed chicken, cucumbers, and tea. More than one undoubtedly believed these kindnesses might be repaid by her husband in the form of cash. That would never happen.

Edwin Lippincott died just after 2 o'clock on the afternoon of July 12, 1890. His doctor pronounced the cause of death as mental worry and anxiety over the actions of his wife.

From the moment he'd learned she absconded, Edwin never spoke badly of Julia, although his family noted that he spent hours silently brooding over her betrayal. The man with the sterling reputation, the man so strong in his religious convictions that he ran a dry seaside hotel, was emotionally and financially ruined by the one person he'd trusted the most; the one person who was absent when he was laid to rest in Friends Acre near the Medford Quaker Meeting House he attended.

While Edwin's remaining family members may have believed that Julia's problems were now her own, they clearly misjudged his widow. Less than a month after his death, Julia contested Edwin's will and his choice to completely disinherit her. She filed suit on the grounds that Edwin's family had exerted undue influence over him. Edwin's mind had been failing for several years, Julia argued, and they took advantage of that to plot against her. Particularly to blame was Isaac Stokes, whom Julia declared "hypnotized Edwin completely."

Seemingly contradicting herself, Julia insisted that, even though he was mentally unfit when he'd disinherited her, Edwin still approved all of the transactions on which she'd signed his name. Meanwhile, she'd hired a second attorney, Howard Carrow, who claimed to have found a piece of land in Atlantic City still owned by Edwin and insisted it be included in the estate and sold, with proceeds going to Julia. Unfortunately for her, this purchase was never substantiated.

After months of lurid newspaper coverage, including daily tales of more and more victims, Julia's New Jersey cases finally went to trial in early December 1890. She testified at all of them, which, clearly, worked in her favor.

Her first jury deliberated seven hours before finding Julia Lippincott not guilty of the charges of forgery. Dressed in her favorite black-and-white color scheme—including her black "walking hat"—Julia confidently exited the courtroom. She fully expected the same outcome at all of her trials, and she was right. Jury number two also acquitted Julia—even though the man she'd defrauded testified that the signature on the promissory note was not his. In frustration, the Camden County prosecutor filed three more indictments against Julia on December 11. It was no use. Each and every time she spoke to the jury, it was as if she hypnotized them into believing her story. After the fifth acquittal, the prosecutor gave up and ordered Julia released from jail. Perhaps Camden believed their southern neighbor Atlantic County would have better luck.

It did not.

For convenience's sake, Julia was housed in a room on the second floor of the Atlantic County sheriff's residence. There, reporters once again freely visited.

"I will pay all my debts once I'm acquitted," Julia told them. "Except to those who took me to court. I also plan to challenge my husband's will." According to Julia, she had every intention of getting the $100,000 to $200,000 of his estate to which she believed she was owed.

After five days of confinement in the sheriff's office, bondsman I. H. Adams was finally convinced to pay her bail, and Julia was released on December 21, 1890. Her trial was moved from April 1891 to September of that year, but this just postponed the inevitable. Even the testimony of Edwin's brother-in-law, the well-respected Isaac Stokes—whose name Julia had forged using the wrong middle initial—failed to sway the jury. Once again, Julia took the stand in her own defense. Once again, she was acquitted.

One might think, considering her streak of freakishly good luck, that Julia might move on to more legitimate pursuits. Two years later, however, she was back in jail, and this time it was Philadelphia's turn at bat.

On Thursday, June 29, 1893, Julia appeared before Magistrate Pole to face the charge of forging Mary A. Haines's name on an $8,000 mortgage. Pole set her bail at $2,000, a sum she could not produce, so Julia was taken to the infamous Moyamensing Prison.

This looked like the case that could finally end Julia's criminal career. It was undisputed that she'd used a life insurance policy as security for the mortgage. Mary Haines denied ever signing that mortgage, and, indeed, the prosecutor pointed out that the "M" in the forged signature in no way resembled Mary's own handwriting.

Sensing a possible turning tide, attorneys R. O. Moon and Howard Carrow tried a new tactic. They argued that the entire case should be dismissed because the statute of limitations had passed. It would have worked had not Julia claimed her state of residence as New Jersey. As was rightly the case, the magistrate determined that the statute of limitations applied only to Pennsylvania residents. In one of Julia's rare unfriendly rulings, Pole proceeded to trial, only to have the Philadelphia jury, once again, decide in her favor.

Whether Julia continued her fraudulent dealings, we'll never know. She appeared in the census one final time, in Baltimore in 1900, where she was living with her sister and brother-in-law. There are no records of her death and no indications that she remarried. The only thing we know for certain is that she isn't buried beside Edwin.

6

KATE SOFFEL, THE WAYWARD WARDEN'S WIFE

She watched him every day from her sewing room in the warden's residence of the Allegheny County jail. Stone walls hid it from the public, but she could see the prisoner courtyard from her window.

He walked outside each afternoon, always with his brother. She couldn't remember when he first caught her eye or why. She wasn't sure when she began to believe that he felt the same way about her. She'd read about his crimes, but she knew the stories were wrong. He'd never steal, much less kill. No, the police, the judge, the jury—they'd all gotten it wrong. It was her duty as a Christian woman to make things right.

She knew she was sacrificing everything. Her husband would never forgive her. Her children probably wouldn't either. These were the prices to be paid. Ed Biddle needed help, and she, the warden's wife, was the only one who could give it.

On this snowy January night, she stood in her darkened sewing room, waiting. A matchlight sprang to life in the cell below. She fumbled in the dark and found and lit her own match. For a brief few seconds, the two flames burned together. Her hands trembled as she blew out the match.

This was the sign she'd been waiting for. This was the night that would change Kate Soffel's life forever, if she survived it.

MRS. SOFFEL WAS A DEMON INCARNATE

It Is Said That She Was Willing to Allow the Murder of Her Husband to Help the Biddles.

MANY EVIDENCES OF HER PERFIDY

Common to that time (and even true today), Kate Soffel was characterized as the demon who led good men astray—even though the men in question were thieves and murderers long before they met the warden's wife.

Katherine Dietrich was born in 1867, two years after the end of the Civil War. It was a war her father, Conrad, knew far too much about. Conrad Heinrich Dietrich served as a private in the 29th New York Infantry, colloquially known as the 1st German Infantry. He had only arrived on American shores nine years before the outbreak of hostilities. Like many German immigrants (who made up the majority of Union troops), Conrad was more than willing to fight for his new country and, in fact, witnessed the bloodiest combat of the war, including both battles of Bull Run. Unlike many veterans, he survived unscathed and moved to Coal Hill (today's Mount Washington) overlooking the smoky, industrial city of Pittsburgh.

The Dietrichs were one of many German families on the Hill, an ethnic group that gravitated toward skilled jobs and professions like mold maker, brakeman, bookkeeper, plumber, and butcher. Conrad was a leatherworker, mainly supplying uppers, soles, and findings to shoemakers like fellow Deutschland emigre Peter Soffel. After decades of owning his own shop,

Conrad and other independent tradesmen were replaced by large corporations. He would take a job as a guard in the county jail, a position Conrad believed would see him through his retirement years.

Like Conrad, Peter Soffel Sr. came to America as a child and built a business on the Hill. He hoped to pass the shoemaking shop to his eldest son and apprentice, Peter K. Soffel. The younger Peter's ambitions, however, were more akin to his uncle Jacob's.

Soon after arriving in Pittsburgh, Jacob Soffel found a job as an interpreter for the county courthouse, translating German to English. This led to the elected position of alderman, an office to which he was handily reelected in 1892. Jacob ended his career in public service as the crier for the Allegheny County Court of Common Pleas.

Likely with Jacob's recommendation, nephew Peter was offered an index clerk position with the Register of Wills office. He was on his way to becoming a well-known and respected man in the community, like his uncle. The only things Peter lacked were a wife and family.

For the Dietrich and Soffel families, the December 9, 1886, marriage of Kate and Peter might have been more of a relief than an arranged union. Peter was young, just twenty-two. Kate was still six months shy of her twentieth birthday. She was neither well-traveled nor well-educated, having left school at age thirteen, right about the time her mother died. If anyone noticed that their first daughter, Irene, was born barely nine months after the marriage, they were polite enough to keep it to themselves.

Three years into their marriage, Peter was named deputy warden of the Allegheny County jail. The new job meant more money, and they could still live in their own home. With Peter's next promotion to warden in 1900, however, the county required that his family—which by now included four children between the ages of five and twelve—move into the warden's residence, an apartment attached to the jail.

The jail in which the Soffel family lived was the county's third. By the late 1880s, its predecessor was considered a blot on Pittsburgh's name. Dangerously overcrowded, it housed dozens of convicts better suited to more secure facilities like Western Penitentiary, or less severe punishment such as the county's workhouse. City officials agreed that a new jail was needed, sooner rather than later. In 1886, the Romanesque Revival–style jail on Ross Street admitted its first inmates.

Pittsburgh's Bridge of Sighs made the convicts' trek from the neighboring courthouse to the jail an easy one. Similar in appearance to its namesake in Venice, this arched bridge witnessed the footfalls of countless men and women being led to their confinement or, worse, execution. Located just steps from the warden's private entrance, Kate was as familiar with it as she was with the prisoner courtyard she watched from her sewing room. During the early part of her husband's tenure as warden, Kate had very little interest in the prisoners for whom Peter K. Soffel was responsible. That changed in the spring of 1901 when she, and most of Western Pennsylvania, learned about two brothers awaiting execution for killing both a grocer on Mount Washington and the police officer sent to arrest them.

It had been a pleasantly warm April in Pittsburgh; there was no substantial rain or snow to speak of and daily temperatures reaching well into the fifties. On the early evening of April 11, Walter Mensinger, an engineer in his family's firm, took advantage of the mild weather to exercise and toss a football with a friend. The sport was still relatively new—in fact, the first professional player had been paid by the Allegheny Athletic Association less than a decade earlier—but it was already a thriving pastime in the Pittsburgh region.

When it came time to head home for the evening, Mensinger noticed something odd: three men, two of whom seemed to be purposely hiding in the shadows, stood idly on the sidewalk. One watched Mrs. Bradley's confection store on Prospect Avenue. The other two appeared to gaze down an alley toward Kahney's grocery store. Perhaps because he noticed that Mensinger had noticed him, the man staring at Bradley's store entered it and purchased several tobies, cheap cigars made of low-quality tobacco. This seemingly normal act did nothing to assuage Mensinger's suspicions. After the men left, Mensinger went inside and warned the young clerk to be cautious if she spotted the trio again.

Had Mensinger known that two of these men were spotted earlier in the day by a neighbor of the Kahneys, he may have alerted the police. Like Mensinger, Lara Essig sensed that something was off about these strangers.

Around 3 o'clock in the afternoon, she took a break from doing the family laundry to go outside to check on her children. She saw two men outside Kahney's store. In a neighborhood where everyone knew everyone, it was enough to pique her curiosity. Twelve hours later, both she and Walter Mensinger would discover the horrible reason for their visit.

At five-foot-ten and 170 pounds, Thomas Donnelly Kahney was not what one might assume to be a pushover. For five years, he and his wife Sarah, whom he called Sadie, owned and operated a grocery store on Albert Street in Mount Washington. The shop was in the front, street-side portion of the building, and their living quarters were in the rear. Like most of Pittsburgh, Thomas had heard of the spree of burglaries happening around the city, a knowledge that served to make him even more cautious than he already was. Thomas had always made it a point to check his shop if he awoke in the middle of the night, and he encouraged his wife to do the same.

Sadie awoke several times during the early morning hours of April 12, 1901. Her son, Earl, was ill and restless. Instead of sleeping in her own bed, she stretched out beside him. Sleep came hard. Sadie would fall into a short-lived slumber, get up and walk around the shop, then return to check on her son.

Just before 3 a.m., Sadie bolted awake to the terrifying realization that someone was pressing a coarse cloth against her nose and mouth. It reeked of chloroform. As she struggled to escape, the liquid spread across her face and dripped down her throat. She could not breathe. Her skin and eyes were on fire, yet she fought the desire to succumb to its anesthetic properties. As she later testified at the coroner's inquest, she also prayed.

Out of the corner of her eye, Sadie saw her son lifting himself from the bed. What would happen if he, too, was chloroformed? Would he fight? Would he be killed? Would she?

With a strength that surprised even herself, Sadie made one last attempt to break free from her attacker. She found herself sideways, half on the bed and half off, able only to see the lower half of the intruder's body. It was a man—which is all she knew. She got a good look at his trousers and shoes and forced herself to remember the details. Then, somehow, she made it to her feet.

Sadie was both relieved and frightened by the squeaking of the bed-springs in the room next to Earl's. It was her husband. She needed his help but feared for his safety. As Thomas opened his bedroom door to enter Earl's room, a sliver of light revealed two more men hidden in the dark. Three men in total. Sadie fought even harder. She shoved the rag from her face and tried to wrestle loose, but her captor kept an arm around her shoulders.

Thomas was in Earl's doorway now. The man detaining her reached for his right pocket. A gun. He was reaching for a gun.

Sadie heard the bang and saw a flash.

Thomas didn't react.

Thank God, Sadie thought, *the bullet missed him.*

"Wait, Sadie," Thomas screamed. "I'll get my revolver!"

Hearing that, the two men in the shadows fled back toward the kitchen window through which they'd entered. Realizing he was now alone, the man gripping Sadie let her go and followed them. As he shoved past her, she could smell chewing tobacco on his breath and saw that he was wearing a false beard.

Thomas ran after the intruders. Once at the kitchen window, he again yelled to Sadie that he was getting his revolver. He turned and ran toward his bedroom to retrieve it. Sadie ran to Earl's bedroom window, threw it open, and screamed for her neighbors to send help.

As he approached his own bedroom doorway, it occurred to Thomas that something was horribly wrong. He felt a terrific pain in his chest. His torso was covered with blood. He turned back toward Sadie.

"I am shot," he told her.

The neighborhood doctor arrived at the Kahney home as quickly as possible, but his haste was in vain. The bullet that killed Thomas Donnelly Kahney had entered his left side between the fourth and fifth ribs. It tore through his lung and heart before exiting through the fourth and fifth ribs of his right side.

There was never any hope of saving the Mount Washington grocer.

News of Kahney's murder traumatized an already fearful community. The string of burglaries had been bad enough. Now that the gang had

BIDDLE BOYS WILL NOT HANG ON THE SAME DAY

Gov. W. A. Stone Writes That the Request of the Murderers of Grocer Thomas D. Kahney Will Be Granted.

MURDERER EDWARD BIDDLE.

The above is a remarkable picture from the fact that it was taken in the jail yard on the spot where Biddle will pay the penalty of the law with his life for the killing of Kahney. The murderer's face is as void of terror as when he heard Walter Dorman's damaging confession in court.

Kate Soffel fell in love with murderer Ed Biddle, then made the even bigger mistake of helping him escape the prison of which her husband was warden.

escalated to murder, it was imperative that the Pittsburgh police find the perpetrators. As it turns out, luck was on their side.

On that Friday, the day of the murder, detectives received reports of suspicious activity occurring at two houses, one on Bedford Avenue and the other on the intersecting street of Fulton. A man and a woman called Mr. and Mrs. Wilcox rented a room on Bedford Avenue. Two brothers named Wright, as well as a woman going by the name Mrs. Wright, were letting rooms on Fulton Street. All were keeping strange late night and early morning hours.

Detective Patrick E. Fitzgerald, known to his colleagues as Paddy, was a forty-five-year-old husband and father when he was tasked with bringing the Bedford and Fulton occupants to the police station. The arrest at 1714 Bedford was swift and easy. Except for Mrs. Wilcox initially attempting to block the entrance to their second-floor room, neither she nor her presumed husband offered any resistance at all. Perhaps the three revolvers that were found under Wilcox's pillow, though, should have been an omen that their second arrest would not be so simple.

After delivering the Wilcoxes to Police Station House No. 2, Fitzgerald, along with Detective Robert Robinson and Inspector Robert S. Gray, went to the rooming house at 32 Fulton Street. Along the way, they passed Officer West, one of Pittsburgh's earliest African American officers, and asked him to stand outside and guard the entrance.

A little girl answered their knock on the rooming house door and let them inside. The landlady, May Smith, was seated in a rocking chair on the first floor. As the police spoke with her, they noticed another woman ascending the stairs to the second floor. Shortly thereafter, a man came up from the cellar kitchen. Asked his identity, he offered the name John Wright.

"You're one of the men we're looking for," Fitzgerald told him before placing him under arrest.

A search of John's pockets produced a revolver but no other weapons. "You stay here with him," Fitzgerald told Detective Robinson.

Fitzgerald and Gray went to the second floor. They knocked on every door, not knowing which was occupied by the second suspect. When a woman responded to their raps by asking who they were, Fitzgerald had a hunch they'd found the right room. He demanded entry. Mrs. Wright opened the door, and both policemen rushed in. Fitzgerald trained his gun on Ed Wright, who fired four or five shots in quick succession. Fitzgerald returned fire. Mrs. Wright fled the room, somehow evading the barrage of bullets.

Even though two of Fitzgerald's bullets had hit their mark, Ed tossed his spent .38 revolver and retrieved a .32 from under his pillow. He resumed firing. In an act of blind courage, Gray charged Ed and wrenched the revolver from his hand. Fitzgerald staggered toward them.

"Are you shot?" Gray asked him.

"Yes," Fitzgerald replied. "I'm all in." With that, he fell face forward to the floor.

At the first sound of gunfire, Robinson had trained his revolver on John Wright and warned him against making any sudden movements. Gray bounded down the stairs to now deliver the news Robinson feared. "He killed Paddy," Gray reported.

"What about Wright?" Robinson asked.

"He's dead, too," Gray replied.

"Good," Robinson said.

Certainly, Ed Wright should have been dead. One bullet took a chunk of flesh from the left side of his face and head, and another was lodged in his right leg. Surprisingly, though, Gray was wrong. Ed was still breathing, and he and his brother had several more surprises up their sleeves.

When first arrested, the three men and two women removed from Bedford Avenue and Fulton Street were identified in newspaper headlines as the "Wright-Wilcox band of robbers." Police were confident that these were the burglars who had been plaguing Pittsburgh and the evidence found in their rooms clearly proved it. Auger bits found among their possessions matched in size to the holes drilled into the Kahneys' kitchen shutters, as did bits of wood found on the auger tips. Small scrapings of green paint on the wood shavings matched the Kahney house. As if this weren't enough, a salesclerk at Standard Supply Company identified Wilcox as the man who purchased the tool.

Footprints in the Kahneys' yard matched those of Wilcox, and eyewitnesses placed all three men in the area just before the murder.

Kate Soffel never escaped the notoriety of the Biddle case. She remained single and died under an assumed name, although neighbors knew the true identity of the quiet seamstress.

Further sealing the case was the trove of stolen items recovered from the boarding houses. The thieves had been brazen enough to ship some of their hauls to other cities and dumb enough to keep the receipts. Dozens of citizens visited the police station to describe and reclaim their valuables. The resulting publicity also led other potential victims to come forward. John Harris, butler to wealthy industrialist W. H. Lewis, told police of three men who knocked on Lewis's front door. They were there, they said, because they mistakenly believed it was the home of a friend. Harris was immediately suspicious and sent them away. Instead of leaving, they crept around back to the home's rear entrance. The screams of the maids, who moments later encountered them while leaving the kitchen, chased the intruders away for good. Harris was positive that two of those men were Wilcox and John Wright.

As to be expected, the murder of a police officer inflamed not only his colleagues but city residents as well. The day after his death, a fund was created for Fitzgerald's widow and children. Initial donations totaled $1,200. That balance tripled within days. Though less noticed by the newspapers, friends and neighbors of Sadie Kahney fundraised for her as well. Even the Mount Washington Thespian Dramatic Company mounted a benefit performance in her name.

Thomas Donnelly Kahney was buried on April 13, 1901. His funeral was held in his sitting room. Dozens of lilies, roses, and carnations sent by sympathetic friends and strangers scented the small space. Attendees overflowed to other rooms of the living area and into the grocery shop.

Patrick Fitzgerald's funeral was held at St. Rosalia's Church on Greenfield Avenue. Pallbearers included both Detective Robinson and Inspector Gray. More than 500 people visited the Fitzgerald family home to pay their respects. Though confined to her bedroom by grief, the widow received messages of condolence from police departments across the nation.

The city mourned collectively. No one doubted that the Wright brothers and Wilcox were the men responsible for this senseless loss of life. No one felt sympathy for them or questioned their arrests.

While Ed Wright recovered in Mercy Hospital, his brother John, accomplice Wilcox, and their two female companions slept soundly in the county jail, using rolled-up clothing and hats as pillows.

Two days after the murders, police learned the women's true identities. "Mrs. Wright" was actually Jessie Mae Bodyne of Hurley, Michigan. Why the petite, attractive dance teacher decided to go on a crime spree with Ed Wright was still a mystery. Jennie Siefer, the supposed "Mrs. Wilcox," was a large woman with round cheeks and long, unnaturally yellow hair. Unlike Jessie, whom police initially believed to be the brains of the operation, Jennie would never be mistaken for an intellectual.

As his hospital discharge and subsequent incarceration drew nearer, Ed's behavior grew more theatrical. Doctors were quite certain that neither of Ed's wounds was life-threatening. They removed a .32-caliber slug from his jaw but left the bullet in his right leg. Removing it would have caused more damage than the shooting had. Though recovering quickly, Ed feigned horrific pain, alternating between high-pitched shrieks and guttural moans. On occasion, he would bolt upright in his bed and claw the air as if fighting invisible attackers. It was one of the rare occasions in Ed's life when he fooled no one.

On April 15, John Wright told police his and his brother's real names: John and Ed Biddle. Why John admitted this information is not known, but it helped police from Pittsburgh and neighboring cities piece together the siblings' crime tour, which included a stint in nearby McKeesport.

Meanwhile, investigators also discovered that "Wilcox" was actually Walter Dorman, the son of a well-to-do family in Cleveland, Ohio. When interviewed, Dorman's parents admitted the twenty-two-year-old was a wild child whose criminal career began with stealing from churches and progressed to robbing houses. Authorities also believed, but could not prove, that Dorman had started a fire in an apartment building that killed a young mother and her baby.

Dorman's "wife," Jennie, hailed from Milwaukee. She was legally married to a railway brakeman named Harry Bradford, whom she deserted for a highly unsuccessful career on the stage.

Two days after learning his real name, police transported Ed Biddle from his hospital room to the courthouse, where he was officially charged with the Kahney and Fitzgerald murders. Dorman and John Biddle were also charged with Kahney's murder. The women faced the lesser charges of receiving stolen property, although these were later dropped.

Though the band of criminals exhibited a pretense of loyalty, rumors were spreading that Dorman was talking to District Attorney John C. Haymaker.

Even before the Biddles went to trial, observant spectators sensed a subtle but perceptible change in public opinion. Newspapermen who initially described the gang as wanton, ice-cold criminals suddenly saw a new side to

Ed. The spiritual advisor assigned to Ed in jail described the accused murderer as being one of the most magnetic men he'd ever met. His charisma bordered on hypnotic, the reverend said. Even prison guards—including Conrad Dietrich—seemed starstruck by Ed. They spoke in glowing terms of his charm and friendly demeanor and, in Conrad's case, openly questioned the brothers' guilt.

The photo most often printed alongside coverage of the case showed the twenty-four-year-old as a dapper, handsome young man. With thick, black hair parted in the middle, a sharply defined nose, and deeply recessed dark eyes, Ed Biddle looked more like a society gent than a cold-blooded killer—a fact not lost on women readers. Female support, even from those who had never met Ed, grew throughout his incarceration.

On April 30, 1901, an Allegheny County grand jury indicted the Biddles and Dorman on two charges of murder and five charges of burglary. D. A. Haymaker announced that John Biddle's trial would commence on June 10; Ed's would be on June 17.

Luckily for the Biddles, their court-appointed defense counsel was James Francis Burke. Described by one contemporary as a "platinum-tongued orator," Burke would go on to become a United States congressman before serving on the cabinet of President Warren G. Harding. Yet, as good of an attorney as he was, Burke's firepower was insufficient against the bomb that fell on the first day of John's trial. It turned out those rumors about Dorman were true.

"Yes, I was there to rob Kahney," Dorman confessed, "but it was John Biddle who shot the grocer."

In total, including jury deliberation, John's trial lasted just four days before he was found guilty of first-degree murder.

The following week, Ed was tried and convicted at the same speedy pace.

In July, Ed argued for a new trial. His request was denied, and the Biddle Boys, as they were now known, were sentenced to death. Walter Dorman was declared guilty of first-degree murder on July 18, 1901, but his death sentence was postponed until all appeals were exhausted.

On August 7, 1901, the Biddles appealed their convictions to the Pennsylvania Supreme Court. Many observers wondered how they financed this legal challenge. The filing fee alone was $12 in an age when the average American worker earned $8.65 per week. As it turned out, their brother Harry—who hadn't seen his siblings in eighteen years—had cashed out most of his and his wife's personal assets to finance Ed and John's legal expenses.

The transcript of the Supreme Court testimony revealed even further evidence of the gang's premeditated ruthlessness. As detailed in the opinion delivered by the justices, not only had Sadie Kahney spotted the men on the street the day of her husband's murder, but Walter Dorman had also spoken to her husband face-to-face.

On the pretense of gathering information for a city directory, Dorman "interviewed" Kahney in his store. The unsuspecting grocer freely shared the fact that his household consisted only of himself, his wife, and their young son. He also described to Dorman his living quarters: a small sitting room, kitchen, and two bedrooms at the rear of the shop. It was all the insight the trio needed to target the Kahneys for a robbery later that night.

The Biddles returned to the street outside the Kahney store between 10 and 11 p.m. They waited several hours to make sure the family was asleep. Ed carried two revolvers. John had a revolver and a club. Dorman carried a revolver and the chloroform with which he unsuccessfully attempted to subdue the grocer's wife. The Biddles wore masks, and Dorman donned a fake beard.

In what was surely his most cowardly act, Ed trained both of his guns on the sleeping, sick child. John stood at the foot of the bed, nearest the entrance to the second bedroom. When Kahney entered Earl's room and announced he was getting his revolver, John shot him at close range.

This testimony—like that heard in the original trial—left little reasonable doubt about Dorman's and the Biddles' ill intent or their murderous natures. Still, once the execution dates were set, newspapers and their readers expressed doubts. Editors accused the police of conducting a "muddled investigation." A popular theory suggested that Kahney's killers were actually Walter Dorman and his stage-actress wife dressed as a man and that the Biddles were just patsies.

No group expressed more ardent concern for the Biddles than women. At the height of their advocacy, no less than twenty-five women visited the

Biddles regularly while working to overturn their convictions. Among this coterie were wives of prominent businessmen, two nuns from the Webster Avenue convent, and the warden's wife, Kate Soffel.

Exactly when Kate and Ed began communicating will never be known. It is almost a certainty, though, that Ed initiated the relationship. If there was one thing the charismatic Ed excelled at, it was knowing exactly what human triggers to pull. As he watched Kate in her sewing room window, something told Ed that he could manipulate her. He was right.

Against the wishes of her husband, Kate began visiting Ed and John in their cell. Ed mournfully expressed regret for the bad things he'd done in his life but swore he'd never hurt anyone.

"I'd never do anything like that," he told Kate. "You believe me, don't you?"

Kate assured him that she did.

Her visits grew in frequency. Guards couldn't help but notice that Kate often came between the hours of 7 and 10 p.m., the time in between her husband's nightly inspections when he rested in the warden's residence. They watched curiously as she and Ed passed a Bible back and forth night after night. The guards knew something was wrong; they just couldn't peg it. As it turned out, the Bible wasn't a means of saving the Biddles' souls—it was a delivery vehicle for sharing coded messages. The Biddles were planning an escape, and Kate was helping them. The signal that they were making their break would be a lit match.

As their February 1902 execution dates drew nearer, the efforts to save the Biddles' lives grew more frenetic. One woman, whom he refused to name, traveled from Pittsburgh to Harrisburg to personally encourage Governor William Stone to pardon the men. Complete strangers of both genders wrote to the judge, with the attorneys and the prison demanding the verdict and death sentence be reconsidered.

What set Kate Soffel apart from the others was her ability to assist the Biddles. While other ladies offered empty sympathetic cliches on scented stationery, Kate was delivering saw blades and revolvers hidden inside her oversized skirts. That she didn't know the purpose of the weapons seems incredibly naive. And what might become of her after the Biddles successfully escaped didn't seem to matter.

When he arrived at the jail the evening of January 30, 1902, James McGarey expected another uneventful overnight shift. Few prisoners were awake, and the jail was quiet. The calm was shattered at 4 a.m. when Ed Biddle's cries ricocheted around the jail like a cannon blast.

"Help!" Ed screamed. "My brother needs help!"

McGarey ran to the Biddles' upper-level cell. John lay on his cot, grasping his midsection and writhing in pain.

"There's something wrong with him," Ed said. "Feel his stomach. There's a lump in it."

When the all-too-trusting McGarey reached through the bars to touch John's abdomen, Ed grabbed his arm. John wedged his way through the jail bars they'd spent the previous days sawing and detained the guard from outside the cell. Ed followed John into the hallway. Together the brothers heaved McGarey over the railing. He fell sixteen feet, landing head-first onto the concrete floor below.

By now, the other prisoners were awake. Some yelled shouts of encouragement; others screamed for the guards. Charles G. Reynolds reached the scene just in time to see McGarey fall. He charged toward the Biddles and tackled Ed. The two men rolled on the floor in hand-to-hand combat. Reynolds felt the piercing ache of a bullet grazing his hip bone. Where had Ed Biddle gotten a gun?

Next to enter the fray was guard George Koslow who grabbed a chair and raced toward the escapees. He raised the chair over his head and was about to bring it down on Ed's skull when John Biddle leveled a revolver squarely at Koslow's face. Koslow, wisely, lowered his makeshift weapon.

Ed and John Biddle led Reynolds and Koslow to the basement level of the jail, a barely lit pit known as the dungeon. They returned dragging the bleeding and semi-conscious McGarey and locked all three men inside.

Using Kate's directions, the Biddles quickly made their way to the warden's residence. She answered their knock and hurried them inside. Peter, no doubt chloroformed at Ed's suggestion, slept soundly as did Kate's four children. The Biddles changed into Peter's clothes. Kate put on her best hat and dress. Together the trio stepped out onto Ross Street.

It was frigid outside, and a snowstorm of historical impact was closing in on the city. The Biddles originally planned to leave immediately for Toledo, Ohio. Instead, they sheltered in an empty house for several hours before boarding a streetcar to Perrysville.

Upon deboarding, it was obvious to all three that Kate could never keep up to the men on foot. It was hard enough for Ed and John to navigate the wind and snow, let alone the petite warden's wife. They spotted a schoolhouse in the distance. Being the weekend, it was empty, and Kate begged to stop. Fortunately, an unlocked window made for easy access. Ed lit a fire in the woodstove. He told her to wait there while he and John went to find a sleigh.

The brothers spotted the Schwartz family dairy farm and believed the chances were good that there might be a getaway vehicle in the barn. Their hunch was right. Ed and John liberated a white-faced mare and sleigh from the stables. It was a beautiful swell-style vehicle (narrow in the front and wide at the back) with black running gear and gold upholstery. Built for two, it would be a tight fit, but robbers couldn't be choosers.

Kate was just beginning to worry that she'd been abandoned when she heard the horse and sleigh approaching the schoolhouse.

Deputy Warden James Marshall arrived for his shift at the Allegheny County Jail at 7 a.m. on Saturday, January 31, 1902. None of the other guards greeted him. Even more troubling, the Biddles' cell was empty. He sounded the alarm and ran to the residence to notify Warden Soffel.

Peter was confused and angry. He'd been warden for less than two years, and there was now a jailbreak on his watch. This wasn't good, he told himself. He threw on his shoes and reached for the empty coat hook. *Where is my overcoat?* he wondered. More to the point, where was his wife?

Unsurprisingly, county officials wanted to know how the two most notorious inmates in the state had escaped the Allegheny County Jail. Peter K. Soffel, remembering the whisperings of the guards, had more than an inkling as to how it happened and knew he had but one choice. At the 3 p.m. emergency meeting of the prison board, he resigned. Before he did, however, Peter requested the resignation of his father-in-law Conrad

Dietrich—an act that no doubt left a bitter taste in the proud old man's mouth.

Whether or not theirs was a happy marriage, Peter was devastated by Kate's actions. Yes, part of it was the obvious end of their marriage. More likely, though, Kate had committed the one sin Peter could never forgive: she'd embarrassed him professionally.

Sympathetic reporters looked on as the distraught Peter transferred his personal belongings from his desk into a basket. "The man who has no confidence in his wife has no right to live with her," he told them. "I can see things now that others saw before. The last lingering hope I had that she might not have had anything to do with this awful calamity has fled. She has betrayed me."

While Peter vented, the county commissioners acted. They, along with the district attorney's office, offered a $5,000 reward for the Biddles' capture, an incredible sum for the time. Authorities were also piecing together how the escape had been effectuated.

During his search for clues as to his wife's whereabouts, Peter found saw blades hidden under newspapers in one of her drawers. Beeswax residue on the jail cell bars explained how guards failed to notice the cuts. As Kate had been the last person to visit the Biddles since their cells were stripped and searched the previous Sunday, it seemed obvious she'd also provided the weapons, either on her person or in the fruit baskets she often delivered.

The Pittsburgh Police Bureau wired descriptions of the trio to every nearby station. Ed was dressed in a dark blue suit, black satin vest, and a stiff black hat. The unique facial wound incurred during the shootout with Fitzgerald extended from his left cheek to the edge of his lip and there was a blue powder mark on the bridge of his nose. John, twenty-eight years old, stood five-foot-eight and weighed 155 pounds. He wore a gray suit and a soft hat. Brown-haired, blue-eyed Kate was the easiest to spot. Only five-foot-four, she was a small woman, but her fancy, plumed hat was highly recognizable. Along with these descriptions came an order from District Attorney Haymaker to shoot the Biddles on sight.

Why the Biddles wasted so much time before heading for the Ohio state line is a mystery. Perhaps they thought they had such a large head start that police would never catch them. Or maybe, as John later lamented, "the woman" slowed them down. In a further act of poor decision making, after stealing the Schwartz sleigh, the three took a room in James Stevenson's hotel in Mount Chestnut. Ed told Stevenson he and Kate were man and wife, and they were given their own room where they stayed for several hours.

Even on their way out of Mount Chestnut, the sense of urgency seemed to elude the trio. John decided that they needed another weapon. On impulse, as they passed the Wagner farmhouse, John insisted Ed stop. He burst inside the home and, holding the daughter at gunpoint, demanded that Mr. Wagner hand over his rifle. Exchange successful, John leaped back into the sleigh only to discover the rifle's chamber was completely empty of ammunition.

By now, Pittsburgh detectives had traveled north to neighboring Butler County, assuming this to be the Biddles' most logical escape route. After consulting with Butler County Deputy Sheriff Thomas R. Hoon, the posse traveled by sleighs to a rise in the road running along the Little Connoquenessing Creek. There they waited anxiously, praying their guess was correct.

The Pittsburgh men were led by Charles "Buck" McGovern, a former close friend of murdered detective Patrick Fitzgerald. With him was Albert Swinehart. Hoon and his deputies accompanied the Pittsburgh men in their own sleigh.

The fierce winter system battering western Pennsylvania worsened. Old-timers remembered it as one of the most damaging snow and windstorms to ever pummel that area of the state. McGovern and Hoon knew that roads would soon be impassable. Temperatures were dropping rapidly, and they worried not only for themselves but also for the horses.

Thoughts of the cold evaporated when the men spotted a sleigh cresting the hill. The true story of the chaotic encounter can never be known. Each of the participants, however, seemed to have his own version of events.

According to McGovern, as soon as the Biddles saw the group of law enforcement officers, Ed drew his pistol and began firing. McGovern and Swinehart emptied their own revolvers, then drew their rifles. The Biddle boys tumbled from the sleigh, their blood soiling the fresh snow. McGovern asserted that the brothers continued to fire, even while injured and lying on the ground. This, he said, was his justification for approaching John Biddle and blasting one last round into his side.

Hoon's testimony (given during an inquest into the events of the capture) depicted a far less heroic version of McGovern. Hoon agreed that it was Ed Biddle who fired the first shot and that everyone in the posse opened fire when he did. He also reported that the Biddle brothers fell, bleeding, from the sleigh. But from there, Hoon's retelling contradicted McGovern's. Both Biddles, according to Hoon, were severely injured and pleading for their lives. Once on the ground, they were no longer firing, and in fact, Ed implored the officers to put away their weapons and let him die. McGovern, nonetheless, approached John and slammed the butt of his rifle into the incapacitated man's skull. McGovern then took a step backward, Hoon testified, and blasted one final, point-blank shot into John Biddle with his Winchester rifle.

After the Biddles tumbled from the sleigh, the terrified horse lurched off the road and into a neighboring field. It made a U-turn, then returned to the scene of the shooting. Kate Soffel lay inside, bleeding from a gaping wound in her left breast. Miraculously, neither she nor the stolen horse was shot by law enforcement during the melee. Kate's gunshot, doctors later determined, was self-inflicted.

Ed suffered two wounds, both made by a .32-caliber revolver, and both were also determined to be self-inflicted. One punctured his chest, the other his abdomen.

John endured the most egregious injuries. He had two gunshot wounds on his right side, near his liver. His right arm was shattered by five bullets. A 41.75 caliber bullet passed through the right side of his pelvis, damaging his kidney. There was also a self-inflicted bullet wound found on the roof of his mouth, but it had caused only superficial damage.

The Biddles were taken to the hospital cells of Butler County Prison; Kate was taken to a public hospital.

Albert Swinehart drove the sleigh that transported the injured Kate. "How are the Biddle boys?" she asked him. Only after that inquiry did she plead with Swinehart to give her love to her children.

"I left my husband and children because I thought the purpose and cause was just," she reportedly told Swinehart. "Ed told me he was innocent, and I believed him."

McGovern wired news of the capture back down to Pittsburgh. Headlines trumpeting the events routinely offered embellished and erroneous details. From the start, editors and reporters targeted Kate. If readers didn't know about their months-long robbery spree and the two murders they'd committed, they might have believed the Biddles were seminary students before meeting the warden's wife.

The tendency to inflict harsher judgment on Kate than Ed and John Biddle played perfectly into an age-old defense known as the Eve Syndrome: men sinned only with encouragement from women. Kate was described as a "demon incarnate" and baselessly reported to be "willing to allow the murder of her husband to help the Biddles." Even Kate's family was fair game. One article reported the unproven allegation that Conrad had aided his daughter in freeing the Biddles by passing secret messages for her—a charge no one involved with the case believed to be true.

As Kate recovered in the hospital, the Biddles' physicians shared their doubts that the brothers would survive. Reporters waited in the hallway to write the inevitable final chapter and were allowed nearly unlimited access to the dying men.

When asked about their failed escape, John told one reporter, "We would not have been captured if we had not stuck to the woman. But we weren't going to leave her in the lurch."

To his last breath, John Biddle swore his innocence in the Kahney and Fitzgerald murders. "I have taken part in many wrong deeds," he told a newspaperman, "but I have never killed any man and was never implicated with anyone who did." It was a brazenly audacious lie considering the fact that he was just one floor down when Ed shot and killed Detective Fitzgerald.

Ed succumbed to his injuries at 7:45 p.m. on February 1, 1902. John died three hours later.

The only person left to stand trial was Kate.

On February 25, 1902, Kate was taken from the Butler hospital to the Allegheny County courthouse, where she was arraigned. During her bail hearing, when asked if he was related to the prisoner, Conrad Dietrich replied, "I am, to my sorrow." Conrad made no secret of the fact that he neither wanted nor intended to help his daughter, but the insistence of his wife (Kate's stepmother) and Kate's siblings left him little choice but to pay her bond.

In March, Kate was indicted on two charges of felonious assault and one charge of aiding and abetting. Had she been convicted of all three crimes, she could have faced sixteen years in jail and a fine of $2,500. The assault charges were subsequently dropped, and on May 5, Kate pleaded guilty to aiding the escape of prisoners. Five days later, she was sentenced to two years confinement in the Western Penitentiary.

Like all prisoners, Kate's intake was documented in a large record book called the Convict Description and Receiving Docket. Kate Soffel was now prisoner number A03509. The thirty-four-year-old wife and mother was described as having a medium fair complexion and medium-dark chocolate brown hair. She weighed 125 pounds, had no distinguishing marks or scars, and was in good physical health. This, the docket noted, was her first conviction.

Two months into her incarceration, a man she had never seen before visited Kate in prison. He served her legal notice that Peter was suing her for divorce.

Though both Biddles were dead and his wife was serving time for her part in the crime, Peter was determined to mete out his own additional punishment. He had, for months, been conducting his own investigation—not for information on the escape but rather for damaging details about his wife. In his divorce filing, Peter claimed that he had unearthed five witnesses: men who would confess to having sexual relations with Kate. And Carl Johnston, Harry Jones, Julius Weld, Michael Roach, and William Muelstein were just the tip of the iceberg, Peter claimed. He'd been assured there were other men, whose names he failed to uncover, who had also been intimate with his wife.

Kate attempted to mount a defense, but it was useless. She was the notorious Mrs. Soffel, and in the view of both the court and the public, Peter was the victim. On October 21, 1903, Peter was granted his divorce.

Once the marriage dissolved, the daily drip of news reports finally dried up, and gossips gradually moved on to other topics. Even Kate's early release—announced just before the divorce was granted—earned a relatively muted reaction. Western Penitentiary's Warden Johnson responded to reporters' questions about this development with paternal platitudes. "She is an exemplary prisoner," Johnson said, "and has never given the least bit of trouble. She's in charge of the sewing department and is willing and cheerful in her duties. She is in good health, suffering no apparent ill effects of confinement."

Kate left prison on December 10. Weeks later, she was back in the headlines. "Mrs. Soffel to act," newspapers announced. "Woman who helped Biddles escape goes on stage!"

During her incarceration, Kate received a variety of visitors—many of them hoping to cash in on her notoriety. One such schemer was Louis Lesser, a talent manager, who convinced Kate to appear in a stage play about the Biddles' escape and her role in it. Lesser went so far as to fund acting classes for the malleable would-be actress, although by all accounts, it was a wasted investment.

A prolific writer of melodramas named Theodore Kremer had copyrighted a play about the case on May 3, 1902, just three months after the Biddle brothers' deaths. Called *A Desperate Chance*, the drama in four acts opened to a lukewarm response in New York on December 22 of that year. "With the exception of 'A Desperate Chance,' written, nailed together or glued up by Theodore Kremer," one reviewer said, "there was absolutely nothing to tempt the palate of play-goers, and even 'A Desperate Chance,' as presented, raised the question of whether it is not, after all, better to imagine the many ills that such a play is heir to rather than suffer them."

Lesser's proposed version of the play would not only star the infamous warden's wife, but it would also use as props genuine artifacts from the shootout. Ads promised audiences glimpses of Kate's blood-soaked handkerchief, one of the posse's rifles, and the sleigh used in the getaway.

Kate surely recognized this as a bizarre choice of careers. She also undoubtedly viewed it as an opportunity to tell her side of the story and earn a decent living while doing it. Pennsylvania towns in which the play was booked, though, were determined to stifle her plans. Self-appointed moral arbiters in editors' offices teamed up with like-minded judges and social groups like the Women's Christian Temperance Union to harass or arrest Kate and Louis Lesser. In some instances, even theater managers who booked the production were arrested. By 1904, Kate's stage career was finished.

Kate had but one skill left by which she could earn a livelihood—one that created no controversies and raised no hackles among the general public. Operating under the fictitious name Kate Miller, she worked in Pittsburgh as a seamstress and dressmaker. Customers went to Kate because of the quality of her work, although few were fooled by the assumed surname. She was obviously the notorious warden's wife who had helped convicted murderers escape the Allegheny County jail. She was also, however, modest, penitent, and good with a needle. She'd paid her debt to society, not just in days incarcerated but also by forfeiting her family. Her neighbors finally gave Kate the one thing she'd always craved: peace.

The people of Pittsburgh, like the rest of the world, had known for years that many diseases were spread by ingesting impure water. By the late 1800s, plans were drawn for a filtration plant to clean the Allegheny River water pumped into many homes. The plant commenced operation in 1905, and neighborhoods throughout the city were, one by one, switching over to clean, decontaminated drinking water. Unfortunately, the roll-out couldn't keep pace with the outbreaks, and 648 typhoid fever deaths occurred in 1907 alone.

On August 30, 1909, a female victim named Catherine Miller succumbed to the disease. She was forty-two years old. Her death certificate described her as a divorced dressmaker and listed her father as Conrad H. Dietrich. The alias fooled no one, and news of Kate Soffel's death and her obituary were published nationwide.

Kate Dietrich Soffel was cremated on September 1, 1909, though urban legends claim that she is buried with her mother in an unmarked grave.

Conrad followed his daughter in death in 1913. In his will, he left each of Kate's children $10.

The Biddles' accomplice Walter Dorman was pardoned on November 1, 1923. His lips trembled as he exited the prison gates, and he clasped his hands in front of his torso as if still cuffed. He died less than a decade after earning this reprieve.

Peter K. Soffel remarried and moved to Ohio. He worked in the railroad industry as a claim and tax agent and also partnered in the creation of a trucking company. A founding member of the Railway Real Estate Association, he served as the keynote speaker for its first convention.

Peter died in his sleep on September 11, 1936, at the age of seventy-two. The first sentence of his obituary described Peter as the "warden of the Allegheny County jail in 1902 when the Biddle boys made their sensational escape." The remaining paragraphs were devoted to his former wife, Kate Soffel, and her tragic fascination with the Biddle brothers.

7

BERTHA BEILSTEIN, THE MAD MURDERESS

October 2, 1898. 3 a.m.

Bertha "Birdie" Beilstein, awake and on edge, paced her bedroom floor and contemplated the terrible act she was about to perform. She paused briefly to consider the laudanum on her dresser. *No,* she thought. *First, the revolver.*

Bertha slowly opened the door that connected her room to her mother's. Mary Beilstein was sound asleep. Bertha crept to the right side of the bed, the side on which her mother still slept all these months after her husband died. It was dark, but the daughter could make out her mother's form.

Bertha placed the revolver squarely against her mother's breast and pulled the trigger. The booming noise awoke Mary but did not kill her outright. In fact, she bolted upright, facing Bertha.

"Birdie!" she said to her daughter. "What did you do . . . ?"

Bertha turned on the lamp on her mother's side table so she could get a better view of the scene. She raised the gun to Mary's face and fired. Her mother fell back, lifeless, onto the bed. Not realizing this, Bertha fired a third and final bullet into her mother. The first step of her plan was complete.

It was now Bertha's turn to die.

She drank the laudanum and then pumped two .22-caliber rounds into her own body. She laid down on her bed to await death.

It did not come.

An hour later, the badly wounded twenty-year-old decided that, since the bullets to the chest and stomach hadn't done the trick, a .38-caliber round to the head would surely end her misery. She placed the gun to her temple and fired. Unbelievably, it too failed to end her life.

Bertha Beilstein had lost a considerable amount of blood—as well as nearly two ounces of brain matter—yet she was still alive six hours later when her brother entered the bed chambers and discovered the carnage.

The Beilstein family was well-known in Allegheny City, today's North Side neighborhood of Pittsburgh. Patriarch John Friedrich Beilstein (who went by Fred) was a prosperous butcher and seller of fresh and smoked meats. His business occupied the two busiest stalls in the Allegheny Market, and there was little doubt the enterprise would continue to thrive upon passage to his sons.

Fred was born in Germany in 1833 and arrived in America at age five. In 1855, he married his first cousin, Mary Beilstein. At that time, this inter-familial union was viewed by many as particularly stigmatic. Several well-known studies of the day suggested that offspring of such marriages could suffer blindness, deafness, or even lunacy. Even today, nineteen states ban the marriage of first cousins. Nonetheless, Fred and Mary enjoyed a conventional matrimonial alliance eventually giving birth to six children: three daughters and three sons. Bertha Augusta was their youngest child, born in 1878.

The Beilsteins were a normal, traditional family—at least until December 18, 1897. On that day, Fred went to Union Depot to retrieve his wife, who had just returned from a visit with family. Upon arrival back at their home on Spring Garden Avenue, the Beilsteins sat down to enjoy breakfast. In the middle of the meal, Fred fell from his chair to the floor, dead before a doctor could even be summoned.

Her father's death was particularly difficult for Bertha. It was no secret she'd been his favorite child. Tall, blond, and blue-eyed, Bertha was a social darling. Like most young women of means, she was well-educated and cultured. She was regularly spotted at parties wearing new and costly gowns. Her outgoing personality made her easy to like and difficult to ignore. Sadly, though, her demeanor changed abruptly after Fred's death. Her spark seemed to die out, and she was often somber. Even a trip to Chicago did not lift the girl from her funk. She returned home with the same despondency she'd carried west.

Reverend J. J. Brubeck lived in the church adjoining, and supported by, the Beilstein family. Upon hearing the first shots, he went to his bedroom window and searched the streets. Nothing seemed amiss and, after scanning the darkness for several moments, he went back to bed. An hour later, a second series of shots rang out. Once again, Brubeck checked the street. It was not until his sister-in-law suggested that the sound came from the Beilstein home that he went to check on the family.

Around 7:30 a.m., Brubeck knocked on Mary's door but received no response. He then moved the short distance down the hall to Bertha's door. The girl answered his knock but only opened her bedroom door wide enough to speak. Brubeck asked if all was well. Bertha assured him that everything was fine. Somehow the girl with three bullets in her torso and a bullet lodged in her brain convinced the reverend to return to his quarters.

Two hours later, Bertha's youngest brother, Edward, arrived at the home. He had taken over the management of the family business and was bringing his mother and sister their weekly supply of meat. When told by the servant that neither his sister nor mother had yet been downstairs, Edward went upstairs to check on them. The scene that met the young man was unimaginably grisly. He found Mary, sideways on the bed, her face disfigured by a bullet. Her nightgown, bedding, and even the wall behind her pillows were soaked with blood.

In the adjoining room lay Bertha. Propped up against her headboard, the girl was alive but unconscious. Edward first noticed the gaping wound to her head, then saw that his sister was also bleeding from the mid-section. Overwhelmed by grief and shock, the young man could barely function. Somehow, though, he made his way back downstairs and summoned three doctors: Walter Ure, Martin J. Stehley, and F. G. Burg.

There was nothing to be done for Mary. She'd suffered three shots from a .38-caliber pistol. One entered the right breast, and another passed through the right groin. The coup de grace entered the right side of her nose, then traveled downward through her neck until it pierced her seventh vertebrae. Death was instantaneous.

Amazingly, Bertha had fired four shots at herself. Two .22-caliber bullets hit her stomach yet somehow missed every major artery. Another tore through her left breast, just missing her heart. The final shot, from a .38-caliber weapon, tore upwards through her brain before exiting the top of her head. Doctors agreed she would not survive the morning.

A fire company captain arrived on the scene, probably having noticed the commotion, and it was he who finally called the police. Police superintendent Henry Muth sent two detectives, James Steel and Thomas O'Brien, to the home. They were joined by another officer and, eventually, the coroner. As the number of strangers in the Beilstein household increased, Edward tried to pry the circumstances from his semi-conscious sister.

"I wanted to die," Bertha told Edward, "but I didn't want mother to be sad about it."

Looking around her bedroom, Edward could see that Bertha's actions were premeditated. A set of clothing in which Bertha wanted to be buried was folded neatly on a chair. On top of the pile rested a note. It instructed her family to cremate her body and how to disburse her estate. Her piano, for instance, was to go to her sister. Her cash assets were to be equally divided among her brothers. The only thing the note failed to address was the actual reason for the murder and attempted suicide.

Nature may abhor a vacuum but gossips love a lack of certainty. It allowed them to fill this void with wild theories like those that sprang up among the Beilsteins' neighbors and friends. One suggested that the two women argued about the control of property left to Bertha by Fred. Another story suggested that Mary disapproved of Bertha's latest boyfriend because he was Catholic. The family denied both rumors, particularly any suggestion that the motive was financial. It appeared that the only thing everyone agreed upon was that Bertha had to be insane at the time of the shootings.

The family buried Mary Beilstein three days after her death. Her service was held at Grace Evangelical Lutheran Church, the church adjoining the family home. Hours before it began, a crowd gathered in the street out front. Some reporters put the number at three thousand. Reverend Brubeck gave a sermon in English. Immediately afterward, the reverend of a nearby

Bertha Beilstein made headlines as the "Mad Heiress" of Pittsburgh, but she was sane enough to escape the asylum and create a new life in California.

church repeated it in German. Neither man mentioned Bertha or the cause of Mary's death.

Bouquets nearly swallowed the altar. Baskets of flowers circled Mary's coffin. A large floral cross of carnations and asters bore a banner reading, "To Our Dear Mother." Beside her lay a pillow with the embroidered words, "At Rest."

Rather than sit in the pews, the family sat behind the pulpit. They gazed outward, past the seven or eight rows of friends and family members they actually knew and onto the hundreds of strangers attending out of nosiness. Another 2,000 strangers awaited them at the family cemetery on Troy Hill.

During the burial, Edward was noticeably distraught. He draped himself across his mother's casket and, midway through the elegy, had to be revived with a doctor-administered restorative.

As per the family's wishes, the grave itself was filled with ferns and flowers to hide the bare soil. As Mary's coffin was lowered into the hole, she appeared to descend into a verdant garden. As the family said its goodbyes, the coroner concluded his inquest. The verdict surprised no one. Mary's death resulted from gunshot wounds delivered by her daughter Bertha. Motive unknown.

On October 19, Bertha awoke to find she could not move her limbs. Dr. Berg attributed the temporary paralysis to the wound in her head. Amazingly, her other wounds were healing, but not the gruesome lesions on her head. For reasons the doctors could not identify, Bertha often broke into screams and also cried out for her mother.

While Bertha's overall condition slowly improved, her family divided Mary's $30,000 estate.

By November, police wanted to know if Bertha's condition had improved to the point where they could transfer her from her home to the jail. Superintendent Muth was worried that, if he didn't incarcerate her, friends or family members might help spirit Bertha away. The district attorney was not as keen to proceed with the prosecution and advised Muth to curb his enthusiasm.

On November 15, 1898, the Beilstein family received more devastating news. Thirty-three-year-old Edward was dead. Passersby found his body draped across the still fresh grave of his mother. He'd gone to the cemetery every day since her burial, but this was his final visit. A note told loved ones he'd taken his own life with poison.

"Break the news gently to my folks but tell my wife last as I am afraid—she cannot stand the shock," Edward wrote.

Unlike his mother, Edward would receive no service at the Grace Lutheran Evangelical Church his family so generously funded. Reverend Brubeck refused to perform a funeral for a suicide. Instead, Edward's service was held at his home.

It was lost on no one that three members of the Beilstein line had died in less than a year. Talk of a family curse began.

As weeks passed, Bertha's crime slipped to the back of many minds. On February 20, 1899, though, the murder of Mary Beilstein came rushing back to the front pages. That is when Bertha was arrested by county detectives and carried away in a closed carriage. The event was anticipated by the family, who had Bertha packed and ready when the early morning transport arrived. She wore a black silk dress and a new ankle-length cloak. Ringlets fell from below her plumed hat, but they weren't real. Bertha had taken to wearing a blond wig while her own hair grew to a length sufficient to hide her scars. She would be held in the Allegheny County jail until a grand jury determined if she would be tried for murder. That decision came in early March. Bertha, it was announced, was one of five prisoners who would face charges of first-degree murder. In the meantime, she would remain in jail, an environment to which she never adjusted. The jail physician prescribed opiates to the young woman who lived in a perpetual state of restlessness, often screaming out for her mother in the middle of the night. The drugs were ineffective, though, and jail staff looked to the upcoming trial as a form of reprieve.

Like most wealthy families, Bertha's had a choice of legal representation. They chose Clarence Burleigh. A former district attorney, Burleigh's claim to fame was his prosecution of the Homestead rioters. This violent battle between these striking steelworkers and the Carnegie Steel Company had dealt a major setback to labor unions. There was little doubt that Bertha's case would require the same kind of creativity and fearlessness Burleigh exhibited in this notorious case. Come May, on the first day of trial it was clear that is exactly what he would bring.

There were, at the same time as Bertha's, two other trials captivating the state and nation. These were the prosecutions of Matthew S. Quay, corrupt Republican party boss of Philadelphia, and Anne E. George of Canton, Ohio, murderer of President William McKinley's brother-in-law. It no doubt pleased the competitive Burleigh immensely that the Beilstein case had, in many newspapers, superseded even these lurid stories. This publicity wasn't accidental. Burleigh's goal from the very beginning was to generate (hopefully) sympathetic headlines.

In his opening statements, Burleigh introduced two shocking defenses. Firstly, he informed the jury that Bertha's parents were first cousins. He would prove, he promised them, that this near-incestuous relationship all but guaranteed Bertha's degeneracy. Should this not be persuasive enough, Burleigh gave the jury a second, equally outrageous reason to exonerate his client: Bertha, he argued, only killed her mother because Spiritualists told her to.

The public got its first look at Bertha seven months after the murder. She was deathly pale when she entered the courtroom, her white pallor in stark contrast to the plain black dress she wore every day of the proceedings. The wig was gone. Her wavy, naturally blond hair was now just long enough to cover the scars left by the bullet. On the first day of trial, the clerk read aloud the charges and asked how she pleaded.

"Not guilty," Bertha said.

"How will you be tried?" the clerk asked.

"By God and my country," came the reply.

"And may God send you a safe deliverance," the clerk said.

Jury selection began immediately. Bertha's lawyers had twenty peremptory challenges. Additional potential panelists could be excused on reasonable grounds. In the end, twelve men were seated, their occupations ranging from caulker to bookkeeper to gentleman. Testimony began within hours of their selection. Clarence Burleigh wasted no time in introducing his strategy.

"Our defense will be a simple one," he said in his opening statement, "founded absolutely on the proposal that no child would go into its parent's room at 3 o'clock in the morning and shoot its parent to death unless that child was insane. We do not propose to show you that this is the kind of insanity which begins a moment before the killing and ends immediately after the commission of the crime. We propose to show you this insanity had a beginning long ago and from a satisfactory cause."

The prosecution set about to prove that Bertha was quite well aware of her actions and even took responsibility for them. District Attorney Haymaker presented an astonishing array of witnesses who simply invited themselves into the Beilstein home the morning of the murder and trudged unhampered through the murder scene. Several relayed conversations with Bertha.

Reverend Brubeck's sister-in-law, Alice Crickenberger, testified that Bertha was quite matter-of-fact in her acknowledgment. "Mother is dead, and I shot her," Crickenberger quoted the girl as saying.

Bertha's cousin, Sophia Beilstein, provided what she said was a word-for-word account of their exchange. "I said 'Birdie, did you do this?' and she said 'yes.' Later, she told her brother—in my presence—'I shot her but my first shot missed. Then I turned up the light and shot her in the face. I turned down the bed clothes and fired once more. Then I felt her heart to see if it had stopped beating. It had ceased, and I knew she was dead.'"

But what was Bertha's motive? According to Haymaker, her mother had learned of an inappropriate relationship between Bertha and a cousin in Chicago named Fred Beilstein, whom she and others called Will. To many observers, this seemed far-fetched, however—particularly considering that Mary had herself married her first cousin. Nonetheless, he called several witnesses who insinuated an improper association, and it was with this impression that he left with the jury when he rested his case.

It was now Bertha's turn to tell her side of the story.

The crowds that demanded entrance to the trial would not be denied. Even with a dozen deputies guarding the entrance, the massive oak doors leading inside the Allegheny County courthouse were torn from their hinges, and several in the crowd were crushed. If Bertha was aware of the mad scene, she didn't show it. During testimony, she absently played with a smelling salts bottle, chewed her nails, or toyed with the fan she carried each day.

The anticipation of the spectators was palpable when Bertha's cousin Will took the stand. They'd been teased by a portion of a letter read into the record by the prosecution. Sent from Will to Bertha's brother Edward, it said: "Birdie wanted consolation and advice from me. She wanted me to set her mind at ease. If she had got my [response] she would not have done what she did. The person in whose hands this letter fell and who kept it from Bertha is more responsible for last Sunday's deed than anyone else on the face of this earth." That person was Mary Beilstein.

Once on the stand, Will, a medical student in Chicago, denied any romantic relationship with his cousin. When asked about their strange habit of communicating via invisible ink letters and special cipher codes, he said they were merely having a laugh. Clarence Burleigh swiftly led Will away from the incendiary rumors and instead toward Bertha's Spiritualist beliefs.

"During her visit to Chicago," Burleigh asked, "did she say she had seen her father?"

"She said she saw him as a spirit," Will replied.

Bertha Augusta Beilstein took the witness stand in the same black dress she'd worn all week. Rather than start his questioning with the events of her mother's murder, Burleigh first raised the sad memory of the death of Bertha's father.

"It was an exceedingly great shock," Bertha said, "one from which I never recovered and never will. I lost interest in everything. I lost sleep. I fell off in weight many pounds. Oh, so melancholy."

Asked about the Spiritualists she'd visited in Chicago, Bertha confirmed her belief in their gifts. "I believe that persons in this world can communicate with persons in the other. I visited two mediums. The first, a Mrs. Cowan, told me that my father was lonely and would not be happy until my mother and I were with him. Nothing entered my mind then about taking my mother's life."

After visiting the second medium and hearing the same message, Bertha testified, she was convinced her father was indeed lonely. It was then that she cut her visit short and returned home. "I did not sleep at all until the night of the killing," she told the jury. She then, calmly, recounted the well-known tale of how she shot her mother and attempted unsuccessfully to take her own life.

To bolster his insanity defense, Clarence Burleigh called Bertha's doctors to the stand. Dr. Ure described in great detail the gruesome wounds Bertha had inflicted upon herself and at one point showed them a piece of skull bone he'd removed from her brain. He also, without hesitation, declared Bertha insane. Yet Haymaker, too, scored points with his cross-examination.

"How did Bertha's insanity originate?" Haymaker asked Ure.

"From a love affair, I believe," the doctor replied.

"When did she tell you this?"

"About a week after she shot herself."

Burleigh next called Dr. Berg to describe Bertha's delusions. "She told me she saw children on the curtains," Berg testified. "She also once imagined she saw a razor half as big as the room. She said one medium told her that her father was lonely and wanted Bertha and her mother to join him in the other world."

When asked to describe her condition shortly before the murder, Berg replied, "She had delusions and melancholia and brooded over a love affair."

Once again, though, Haymaker was able to undercut some of the emotional impact of the doctor's testimony. "What kind of insanity does Bertha have?" he asked Berg, who was forced to admit he could not name a specific condition.

On Friday, May 12, 1899, it was time for the jurors to do their jobs as fact-finders. The judge instructed them to first consider twenty-two-year-old Bertha Beilstein's defense of insanity. If they indeed found her to be insane, it was their obligation to acquit. If, on the other hand, the jury believed her to be sane, she must be found guilty of murder. At 6 p.m., the twelve men left the courtroom to deliberate.

Lawyers, spectators, and members of the press were aligned in their belief that the jury would likely not deliver a verdict of murder in the first degree. Although Bertha confessed to the crime, it was presumed the jury would return fairly quickly with a determination of second-degree murder or even manslaughter.

At 8 p.m., the judge called the jurors to the courtroom to learn their progress. To everyone's surprise, there was no verdict. They were sent back to their sequestered quarters above the courtroom.

On Saturday morning, the jurors returned. The courtroom was so packed that some spectators climbed on the windowsills to get a view of the proceedings.

The verdict came down at 9:45. Not guilty by reason of insanity.

Bertha's dispassionate expression never changed, even when she was ordered back to jail to await transport to the Western Pennsylvania Hospital for the Insane at Dixmont.

Pennsylvania was the first state to provide care for the insane. The Commonwealth eventually established four hospitals dedicated solely to this purpose. An 1869 law mandated that the opinion of two physicians "of acknowledged respectability," who examined a patient within six days of determination, was required if a man or woman was to be declared mentally incompetent. By the time this lunacy law was passed, though, all four facilities were already overcrowded due to the loose definition used previously. Insanity by intoxication was a favorite diagnosis, as was insanity brought about by epilepsy. "Moral insanity," another term for homosexuality, was also a reason for commitment to an asylum. Paupers, once shut away in poor houses, also became wards based on these conveniently lenient requirements.

Dixmont was named for pioneering reformer Dorothea Dix. After a tour of Europe's prisons and institutions, she returned to America as an impassioned advocate for proper asylums and care of the mentally ill. Dr. Henry A. Hutchinson, Dixmont's superintendent, was less solicitous than Dix, however. He was particularly disdainful of patients like Bertha, the progeny of first cousins.

"Bertha Beilstein is not only insane but also a moral degenerate," he said, referencing her parentage.

Upon arriving at Dixmont, Bertha was impressed by its beautifully landscaped grounds and gardens and the picturesque view of the Ohio River over which the massive structure looked. Still, it was a facility originally built for 600 patients and, by the time of Bertha's admission, there were 950. Two months after her arrival, reports surfaced that she was "steadily gaining

Mary Beilstein was killed by her own daughter, Bertha, who claimed Spiritualists had convinced her to perpetrate the murder.

in flesh," a sign of hopelessly incurable insanity, according to her alienists (an archaic term for psychiatrists). Whether friends and family agreed with this diagnosis is impossible to know, for they were prevented from visiting Bertha.

"In my opinion," declared Dr. Hutchinson, visitors do more harm than good in ninety-nine cases out of one hundred. Under no circumstances will anyone be permitted to see her." His decree did not, of course, stop callers from trying. As many as half a dozen would-be visitors arrived at Dixmont each day, all of them eventually turned away. Some told staff they were relatives. Others suggested they were friends whom Bertha was waiting to see. In reality, they were strangers only interested in learning the most salacious and personal details such as Bertha's style of dress in the asylum, if she'd changed her hairstyle, and what books she read.

Less bold observers were content to watch from a distance. Many waited each day to view the female patients as they walked the lawn. Several patients were misidentified as Bertha, resulting in a brief flurry of erroneous newspaper mentions. Bertha, in actuality, never walked with the other patients and only enjoyed the fresh air outside of normal visiting hours.

In December 1899, Dixmont held its first Christmas masquerade ball. There was a large tree surrounded by gifts from friends and family members, and the event culminated in a turkey dinner. Sixty patients were dressed in costume, but Bertha was not one of them. She declined by explaining she was in the middle of reading a book and still mourning her mother.

Shortly after the holidays, Bertha reached her three-month anniversary of detention in Dixmont. It was significant in that three months was the minimum stay required before a patient could be released. Several friends and family members suggested Bertha was completely recovered and should be released. Her brother-in-law, N. A. Voegtly, disagreed. He demanded a hearing based on his assessment that Bertha was deprived of reason and unable to manage her own affairs and finances.

Hutchinson agreed with Voegtly and, at the hearing, testified that he'd seen no improvement whatsoever in Bertha. When asked for an example of symptoms of mental illness, he relayed this less than damning story:

"She will take from the table a gingersnap or piece of bread and butter, wrap it up carefully in a newspaper, carry it to her bed, and hide it so that the nurse would have to tear the bed to pieces to find it."

Dr. Hutchinson admitted that Bertha had never attempted suicide, but he assured the judge that she spoke of it. He also listed as odd behavior the fact that she refused to attend entertainment events, locked her door, and stayed in her room.

"In my opinion, she is a degenerate," Dr. Hutchinson concluded. "She was born that way and has always been a creature of low moral instincts." His findings, said Dr. Hutchinson, were largely influenced by her family history.

Bertha was not allowed to attend the hearing, but the six jurors did visit her in Dixmont. The next day, they rendered their decision. Bertha was still insane.

By December 1901, Bertha was seemingly far more comfortable and social than when she'd first arrived. The local newspaper went so far as to call her "the belle of the ball" at the Dixmont Christmas dance. Three months later, though, Dr. Hutchinson declared that not only was she still insane, but he also now held no hope of her recovery.

Five years later, after nearly seven years of confinement, Bertha took her fate into her own hands. She wrote a letter to the Department of Charities and Corrections asking to be released. Once again, brother-in-law Voegtly— who was now living in Bertha's family home—fought her emancipation. He was joined by another brother-in-law who had assumed control of the lucrative meat business. But while her family celebrated another legal victory, Bertha was concocting a new strategy. On September 23, 1906, she climbed down the fire escape in the rear of the building and disappeared.

Theories about exactly how Bertha had escaped were as varied as they were entertaining. One suggested that Bertha's wealthy friends bribed staff to let her simply walk away. Another detailed an abduction by Spiritualists. A third alternative suggested that Bertha had actually died and the escape story was a cover-up to allow Dixmont to avoid scandal. These rumors would likely have been far less plentiful had the institution not had a reputation for regularly losing patients. Indeed, Bertha's was the fourth escape in as many months, and her story was a made-for-headlines event. "Mad Murderess Makes Escape!" cried the *Philadelphia Inquirer*, a newspaper on the opposite side of the state. The stories in Bertha's hometown Pittsburgh newspapers were even more melodramatic.

Dr. Henry Hutchinson took the lead on the investigation—an unusual step for a doctor and non-investigator. He'd received a tip that Bertha was in New York hiding at the home of a friend. For three weeks, he searched the streets where he'd been told he could find her. His uninvited visits to Bertha's acquaintances grew tiresome, and his doggedness was futile. Never one to admit his own failures, Dr. Hutchinson publicly insinuated that the person who sent him to New York likely purposely deceived him. He tried a new approach: a reward to anyone who would return Bertha Beilstein to the asylum. The Perkins Union Detective Agency, to whom Dr. Hutchinson first broached the reward, promptly refused the case. If Dr. Hutchinson wanted to retain their services, they said, he would have to pay their standard fees. To head off any similar proposals, the Pinkerton Detective Agency also clarified its policy of refusing cases compensated on a reward basis. As for the police, they delivered a public statement saying they were not working the case. It seemed the only people interested in actually finding Bertha were Dr. Hutchinson, his superiors (who knew nothing about the escape until reporters asked for statements), and Bertha's family.

Implying that he believed Bertha hadn't escaped but rather killed herself, Dr. Hutchinson had the Ohio River dragged for her body. "She never expressed a desire to leave the institution," he explained, "but she often spoke of suicide."

Meanwhile, anonymous sources reported that Dr. Hutchinson knew Bertha's body would never be found because he actually *did* find her in New York. But, because there were no pending charges filed against her, the state refused to initiate extradition proceedings.

By October, Dr. Hutchinson's views unexpectedly evolved. At a meeting of the executive committee of the Western Pennsylvania Hospital for the Insane, he declared, "The patient was apparently in her normal condition and I have, for some time, considered the advisability of consulting the judge regarding her discharge." It was a far cry from his July opinion that Bertha was not "in a fit condition to be at large." Dr. Hutchinson concluded his statement by announcing he was no longer searching for Bertha Beilstein. Others, however, never gave up the hunt. She was in Johnstown, one eye-witness reported. Or was it Pittsburgh? Surely the escapee was in Cleveland, newspapers asserted, after Perkins detectives were spotted there making unannounced and ill-timed visits to a tall, blond German girl who had just given birth to a baby boy.

In May 1907, word was spread that Bertha, using the alias Edna Barker, was on a transatlantic steamship accompanied by a dozen friends. British and German authorities were asked to be on the lookout, and expectations were high that Bertha would be arrested as soon as she landed—although on what charges, no one seemed to know.

In the end, Bertha would fool everyone.

The first announcement came a week after the near universally accepted story that Bertha had sailed for Europe. After all the fuss, all the twists and turns, it seemed . . . well . . . anticlimactic.

"Bertha Beilstein is Dead," read the headline. And she'd been dead for three weeks!

She didn't die in Cleveland, or Pittsburgh, or Johnstown—or even in the river running in front of the insane asylum. She died in Los Angeles, where she'd been living under the pseudonym Olga Miller and working as a waitress in a hotel restaurant. No one was more surprised than Bertha's family, who first learned of her death two weeks before it was announced publicly. Their biggest concern was actually verifying that the dead girl was Bertha. This was necessary before her estate could be settled.

As it happens, one of N. A. Voegtly's best friends, Albert Reineman, was on a business trip in Pasadena. Reineman agreed to travel the fourteen miles to Los Angeles to view the body and confirm Bertha's identity using details provided by Voegtly. It took little time for Reineman to reach his conclusion. "Your description tallies exactly," he told Voegtly in a telegraph, "except for the brown hair." The truth of Bertha's escape from Dixmont could now be divulged.

Some months prior to her escape, Bertha developed a friendship with one of the nurses. The nurse felt Bertha was being held unjustly. She gave her patient cash for the train to Chicago and a key to the fire escape. It took some time for Bertha to work up the nerve to actually use the key, but when she did, her departure from the supposedly secure facility was surprisingly easy.

A guard circled the building every thirty minutes. Bertha watched and waited until he rounded the far corner of the building before descending the iron stairs and making her way down the long lane leading to the street. There, she waited nervously for the next streetcar, which the well-dressed patient boarded without so much as a second glance from the conductor or other passengers. She didn't know her destination, which, coincidentally, turned out to be the neighborhood where her mother was buried. Unbelievably, Bertha decided to visit her mother's grave before fleeing the state. She stood over Mary's gravesite for some time, completely undetected, before boarding a train to Chicago. It was another decidedly uneventful journey for the polite, young woman who raised absolutely no suspicions.

Once in Chicago, Bertha had a choice of visiting her brother Fred or a family friend, the mother of Edmund Wander. She chose the latter. Mrs. Wander opened her door to find Bertha soaked to the bone and chilled by the frigid Chicago rain. While Bertha warmed herself, Edmund and Fred pondered their next steps. They decided that Bertha should leave for the West Coast, where she could live with yet another member of the Wander family. Together, the two men purchased a train ticket, and each also gave Bertha $50 cash. Bertha didn't want to stay in Los Angeles—she simply wanted to work there for a year to prove her sanity before returning to Pittsburgh. Together with Wander, Bertha chose her alias: Olga Miller. It was the name she also used to write letters to Wander, apprising him of her progress and daily life in California.

Six months after arriving in California, Bertha met a book agent by the name of Richard Hardy. Hardy, who swore he had no idea who Bertha was, was instantly smitten by the attractive and cultured blond. He proposed marriage and opened a bank account for her with an initial $58 deposit. As fond as he was, her physical condition was cause for concern.

"She suffered terribly from headaches," he later recalled. "At times, she became delirious and spoke incoherently."

By May 1907, Bertha was ready to give up the alternate reality she'd created on the West Coast and return to Pittsburgh to claim her share of her mother's estate. In a letter to Wander, she wrote, "I fear being caught and placed among those lunatics." It was the last letter she would write.

Bertha Beilstein was found dead in her bed in the Rosslyn Hotel on May 21. Because he was last seen bringing her a glass of milk, Richard Hardy was arrested on suspicion of poisoning Bertha. Her autopsy quickly disproved foul play. A large tumor on the brain had caused her death. Whether it had developed prior to the shooting or if it resulted from the brain injury could not be determined.

As seemed to be a pattern with the Beilsteins, the disposition of Bertha's remains came down to money. Specifically, Mary Beilstein's money. Bertha's brother Fred wanted her remains cremated and returned to Pittsburgh for burial. Worried this might delay the processing of her estate, Bertha's brother-in-law, N. A. Voegtly, insisted that the body be brought to Pittsburgh by train for official identification. Working in conjunction with the Equitable Trust Company, Voegtly received authorization to pursue this latter course of action.

Nearly six weeks after her death, Bertha's coffin arrived back home. Her body was remarkably preserved and easily identified by the four witnesses organized by Voegtly, in addition to himself.

On July 5, 1907, the following news item appeared in the *Pittsburgh Post*:

"Death Notice—On Tuesday, May 21, 1907, at Los Angeles, California, Bertha August Beilstein, daughter of the late J. E. and Mary M. Beilstein of Allegheny, Pennsylvania. Interment strictly private."

At least one family member was not as circumspect as this vaguely respectful death notice might suggest. When news broke that Bertha might be dead, an "unnamed relative" made a very public comment: "Bertha was a strange girl, and her life has been stormy and painful for herself and her friends. I sincerely hope she is dead for her sake and for ours."

On November 26, 1907, relatives split $718.20—the balance of Bertha's estate, less expenses.

8

HELEN BOYLE, HEARTLESS KIDNAPPER

I f the term had been around in the early twentieth century, "wild child" would certainly have applied to Anna McDermott. Born in 1887 to a fireman father and gentile, upper-middle-class mother, Anna wanted nothing more than to leave her comfortable, predictable life behind. Anna dreamed of adventure. Money. Danger. Edward Schaeffer, whom she'd married at the age of eighteen, didn't provide any of that. It wasn't until she met James H. Boyle, native son of the town of Sharon on Pennsylvania's northwest boundary, that Anna knew she'd found her man. James wasn't particularly bright or exciting, but he'd do anything she asked him to do.

Anna was fond of aliases. Over the years, she'd deployed the prefix "Mrs." for a number of men she never married (several of whom probably never even existed), including Frank Parker, Frank Yorke, Frank A. Minor, R. G. Faulkner, and R. G. Walters. It was no surprise, then, that she quickly assumed the alias "Mrs. Boyle" upon meeting James. But a new given name seemed appropriate as well, so Anna—who long fancied herself a lookalike for the then-popular actress Helene Falkner—chose Helen.

Helen Boyle was a natural redhead with a petite build, heart-shaped face, and full lips. Her eyes, always seemingly wide open, dominated her other features. She was stylish and purchased a new wardrobe at every

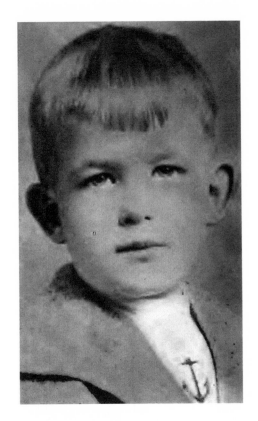

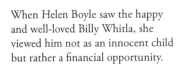
When Helen Boyle saw the happy
and well-loved Billy Whitla, she
viewed him not as an innocent child
but rather a financial opportunity.

opportunity. Helen's good taste, however, was limited by her distinct desire
to avoid a traditional job. That is where James came in.

Like Helen, James had a history of poor decision-making. When he
met Helen in the spring of 1908 in a wine room in St. Louis, Missouri, he
was immediately smitten. Boyle was a plumber by trade, a thick man both
in build and intellect. He was a man of few words—which suited Helen
perfectly, since she always fancied herself the star of the show. On occasion,
Helen would speak French, or at least words she believed to be French. For
those who didn't know better, the vivacious, stylish woman was the epitome
of culture and intellect.

Helen shared with Boyle stories of her past relationships. While he
didn't like hearing these details, he took them as a lesson. Unlike Helen's

previous boyfriend, Frank Parker, who had gone to jail for forging checks, Boyle swore to never let her down.

The couple moved to Springfield, Illinois, in the fall of 1908. With money running out and no good plans to replenish it, Boyle suggested they go back to his hometown of Sharon and enjoy an extended visit at his mother's home. They arrived at the modest home on Orman Avenue on Thanksgiving Day. Boyle introduced Helen as his wife, and his mother had no reason to doubt her son's story.

One afternoon, as Boyle and Helen were taking a walk through town, they came upon the mansion built by steel magnate Frank H. Buhl. Constructed in 1891, the grand sandstone home was magnificent in both size and design. The architect, Charles Owsley, had previously created public buildings like the Mercer County Courthouse. He brought those same dynamic lines and attributes to the Buhl family home.

Helen, like most passersby, was first drawn to the house by its huge, arched porch protecting the oversized front door. The rounded, two-story turret to the right of the porch drew her eye upward to the dormers and finials and copper-laden spires. *Yes*, she thought, *this is what I deserve. It should be me living here.*

The appearance of a small, fair-haired child interrupted her reverie. She assumed it was Buhl's son. He was slight, almost fragile, but clearly felt at home in the large front yard. He looked well-tended and well-to-do. He looked, Helen decided, like an opportunity.

Helen, sometimes with Boyle and sometimes alone, spent weeks studying the home. They quickly realized the child was not Buhl's but rather belonged to the family across the street. Since everyone in town knew Buhl, it didn't take much effort to learn that the boy, Billy, was his beloved nephew—the son of his wife's sister. The two families seemed to share the child, and Billy was nearly as fond of his aunt and uncle as he was his parents. To Helen, that meant he was twice as valuable. She hatched a plan and shared it with Boyle. Whether or not he thought it would work was secondary to his desire to never disappoint the woman he loved.

On March 12, 1909, Boyle and his "wife" said goodbye to his mother. They were going to Denver, they told her, where work was waiting. In actuality, they took a train to Cleveland and rented an apartment in a building called The Granger. They had the alibi. They had the hideout. All they needed was the boy.

By March 18, 1901, winter had relinquished its grip on Mercer County. An hour due north, the last of the Lake Erie ice was melting, and harbors were reopening. On that Thursday morning, Billy's father, a well-known Western Pennsylvania attorney, left for a business trip to Wilmington, a Pennsylvania town about fifteen miles southeast of Sharon. Shortly after James Whitla's departure, Billy ran across the street to kiss his aunt goodbye before biking to his East Ward schoolhouse. Billy's bowtie and knickerbocker suit were clean and new. His little legs pedaled swiftly. He planned to return home at noon for lunch, as he always did.

Isabella cleaned the breakfast dishes and tidied the kitchen, then moved on to the rest of her daily routine. The Whitla home was far less opulent than her sister, Julia Buhl's, mansion, but it was quite comfortable by middle-class standards. The Whitlas lacked for nothing and, unlike many Americans, had weathered the financial panic of 1907 with little loss. Isabella had no reason to believe her easy, predictable life would ever change.

But then, the clock struck twelve, and Billy was not home.

Isabella waited a moment or two inside the house before stepping onto the front porch. Billy, as children do, likely got sidetracked by something or someone he'd seen on the way. Surely, she'd soon see him pedaling furiously toward her. She looked in both directions. The street was empty.

Isabella forced herself to remain calm as she dialed her sister's number. Julia said she hadn't seen Billy since earlier that morning. Next, Isabella called the home of Billy's best friend. Mrs. Southard hadn't seen him either. Now determined to find her son, Isabella donned her hat and coat and walked the same route Billy took to and from school. She didn't encounter him on the way there, and he wasn't in the kitchen waiting for her upon her return.

Isabella called the school. The janitor, Wesley Sloss, answered the call. Billy had arrived safely at school that morning, he assured Isabella, but his father sent a buggy for him about an hour after classes started. In fact, the buggy driver had presented a note from Billy's father at about 9:30, the janitor said.

It took a few moments for Isabella to realize that the story she was hearing couldn't possibly be true. Her husband had left on his business trip well before Billy left for school. And why would he send a buggy for Billy without telling her? Perhaps the janitor was thinking of some other boy. Isabella called Billy's teacher to learn what she knew. To the mother's horror, the teacher told the same story. The note, Anna Lewis told Isabella, said that William Whitla was wanted in his father's office. Billy did, indeed, head off in a buggy driven by a heavyset fellow with a large, black mustache. Its side curtains were closed, and the tires and undercarriage were covered in mud. By the time Isabella learned these details, Billy had been missing for nearly three hours.

Billy's sister Selina had now returned home for lunch to find her mother nearly hysterical. Selina ran next door and returned with her aunt Julia.

"Is it possible that James took a later train?" Julia asked Isabella.

"No," Isabella insisted. "I know when he left."

There was no question that James Whitla needed to be informed of events. Isabella's first thought was to telegraph his office but decided that a faster, long-distance call was required. She was in the process of placing it when the doorbell interrupted. It was the mail carrier. He handed Isabella an envelope. Her heart leaped into her throat when she noticed that the address was written in Billy's handwriting. She tore it open to find the following note inside:

We have your boy and will return him for $10,000. Will see your advertisements in the papers. Insert in Indianapolis News, Cleveland Press, Pittsburgh Dispatch, Youngstown Vindicator: *"A. A.—will do as requested.—J. P. W." P.S. Dead boys are not desirable.*

Isabella nearly collapsed to the floor. She made it to the nearest chair with the help of the mailman. Julia was equally overwrought. Only the teenage daughter, Selina, had the presence of mind to send a telegraph to her father and leave a telephone message for her uncle, Frank Buhl, at his nearby steel plant. Buhl reached the Whitla home within minutes.

Though instantly hated by the American public, Helen Boyle clearly enjoyed the fame the kidnapping of Billy Whitla generated.

The knock on the door startled Helen. Boyle was late in returning to the apartment with the boy, so she was already anxious. She opened the door just wide enough to recognize the telegraph courier. "Telegram for Mrs. Walters," he announced.

Helen snatched the message from his hand and slammed the door. For the first time that day, she breathed a sigh of relief.

"Missed train. Everything O.K.," the message read. It was signed "R. G. Walters."

They had Billy Whitla, and he was on his way to Cleveland with Boyle. Helen ran to the bedroom, where she put on a white dress and apron. Using rouge, she carefully painted red freckles around her face, making sure to remember their placement so she would do it the same way each day.

While James Whitla made his way home from his business trip, Frank Buhl assumed control. He assured Isabella that Billy would be fine as long as they paid the ransom—which he had every intention of doing. Buhl placed the newspaper ads, as the ransom note demanded. He also notified the Sharon Police Department and others of the kidnapping. Lastly, he placed a call to his friend G. B. Perkins, owner of the Perkins Union Detective Agency of Pittsburgh.

In the days before there was a Pennsylvania state police force, railroads, mine operators, and steel mills employed their own private police forces. That was how Buhl and Perkins met: it was Perkins's men who guarded Buhl's steel plant. With regards to Billy, Buhl gave one simple command. Perkins was to use as many men as he thought necessary to see that the little boy was returned unharmed and that the kidnappers were caught.

Upon James Whitla's return home, Buhl met him on the front porch. He quickly updated Billy's father on the events to date and assured him every possible measure had been taken to retrieve the child.

For Buhl, taking charge of things came as naturally as breathing. He had always been the one people turned to to take control. Part of it was his imposing size. Most of it was his unfaltering sense of self-confidence. Buhl was, in short, the opposite of James Whitla.

Whitla was as slim as Buhl was barrel-chested. He was an anxious man prone to nervous retreats inside his own thoughts. His world revolved around a routine. The kidnapping of his son was not something he had ever imagined might happen. It required a steely nerve he simply did not possess. Whitla gratefully accepted the counsel of his brother-in-law.

"We'll get him back," Whitla repeated after Buhl. "We'll get him back."

While Buhl had informed police of Billy's kidnapping, he did not tell them about his plans to pay the ransom. If all went well, the police wouldn't know about that until the family made the drop, retrieved Billy, and turned the kidnappers over to the Perkins detectives. There was but one critical detail that remained missing. The kidnappers had yet to respond to Buhl's ad to tell him where to drop the money.

By late in the evening of March 18, the Whitla family decided to make an attempt at sleep. Before she went to bed, Isabella placed a lamp in the front window of her home. It cast a soft glow onto the sidewalk. James didn't have to ask his wife the reason. He knew the lamp would burn until Billy's return.

Whether spurred by the need to feel useful or the desire to be famous, prominent cases bring out a brigade of bystanders hoping to become the heroes of the investigation. This seems especially true when the life of a child is at stake. When word of Billy Whitla's kidnapping spread, everyone from neighbors to strangers attempted to insinuate themselves into the search. Outraged residents of Sharon inspected empty houses and barns on the chance the boy and his abductors were still in the area. Rural farmers scouted the fields with hunting dogs and lanterns. Every chicken coop, every haystack, every barrel was tossed or overturned.

Mercer County's district attorney requested assistance from the Pennsylvania Mounted Police. The company of officers that searched for Billy had previously been tracking members of the Black Hand, whom most onlookers assumed had taken the child. At the time of the Whitla kidnapping, the disparaging nickname for this relatively new statewide uniformed force was "Pennsylvania Cossacks," and with good reason. It had originally been created to aid the coal and iron police in quelling labor disputes. It wasn't until 1923, when Governor Gifford Pinchot eliminated "company police," that the state police became the impartial law enforcement agency it is today.

The small town of Sharon was overrun by Perkins detectives, adding to the army of citizens looking for Billy Whitla. All outbound trains were searched. Telegraph company linesmen were ordered to be on the lookout, as were the men patrolling the hundreds of miles of Western Pennsylvania gas pipelines. The search expanded to Ohio and states further west. Yet somehow, Helen and James Boyle successfully secluded themselves in plain view in Cleveland.

James Boyle was shocked that Helen's plan had so easily succeeded. The note he presented to the school wasn't even questioned; the teacher sent the boy outside to his carriage without so much as a wave to the driver. Likewise, Billy accepted the kidnappers' story without resistance. Billy's father wanted his son protected from smallpox, Boyle explained, so Billy was going to a place where he could escape confinement in the "pest house."

Billy had likely heard stories of these notorious pest houses. Patients were sent there on the pretext of treatment and humane care. Instead, most of them received indifferent attention at best and complete neglect at worst. The promised medical treatment often never came. The sanitized, freshly laundered bedding and clothing rarely materialized. Pest houses lived up to their name, treating inmates simply as a burden on the healthy society at large.

Billy knew James Boyle as Mr. Jones, an alias shortened to Jonesy. He apparently didn't fear his captors. He did as they instructed him to do and, in return, was treated kindly. He also received repeated doses of ether, in which the candies Helen constantly fed him were soaked.

While Billy waited for his father, whom Helen and James told him would be retrieving him as soon as it was safe, his parents frantically worked toward his return. Police worked around the clock. The same day Billy was snatched, officers found the buggy used to carry him away. The riderless rig was wandering the streets of Warren, Ohio, about twenty-five miles southwest of Sharon. The small steel town immediately became the focal point of the search. Having a target was good news, but it didn't make up for the troubling fact that midnight came and went with no response to Buhl's newspaper ad.

The morning after the abduction, trains and streetcars delivered an army of private Perkins detectives to Warren's streets. They discovered that the buggy was owned by a liveryman named Frank Loveless. Loveless had rented the carriage to a man who said he was a bill collector who needed it to make his rounds. Loveless described the man as broad-shouldered and of medium height with a red face and funny-looking mustache. A second witness, a barber, said he shaved a similar-looking man, although the mustache was missing. Surprisingly, though, not one witness came forward to tell investigators about the lumberyard where James hid Billy while he went to check the train schedule.

While Frank Buhl supervised the work of his Perkins men, James Whitla admitted to police he planned to pay the ransom with no eye toward punishing the kidnappers, assuming Billy was returned safely. Officers in charge of the case strongly discouraged this approach, a warning Buhl both disparaged and ignored.

"Just get the boy," he ordered his Perkins detectives. "That is all I care about."

While the men dealt with the investigation, Isabella desperately waited at home for any word of its progress. On Friday at noon, the postman arrived at the Whitla residence with another envelope addressed in pencil in Billy's handwriting. The letter inside was brief:

"We have seen your advertisement and conclude you mean to play square. Be ready to act upon further instructions."

For the Whitlas and Buhls, this was both a relief and a torment. Billy was presumably still alive, but why hadn't the kidnappers told the family how to pay the ransom?

Upon hearing of the letter, police once again surfaced the first leads. They found the Cleveland mail carrier who originally pulled it from the mailbox at the corner of Payne and East Eighteenth Streets. This seemed to the police to be a blatant and sloppy mistake. Why make the location so easy to find? Suddenly, a new concern surfaced. All along, law enforcement assumed the kidnappers were professionals, perhaps even members of the Black Hand. But what if they weren't? What if they were just amateur opportunists? And if *that* was the case, what would happen to Billy if they felt the pressure of the law closing in on them?

While Helen and James may not yet have realized how closely the police dogged their trail, they did realize that their kidnapping of the boy had sparked public outcry. Rewards were piling up for Billy's return and their capture. Pennsylvania offered $15,000 for the child's recovery. Various newspapers offered their own rewards, payment of which, of course, was contingent on exclusive stories from the winners. In total, the pot now stood at $30,000. While James felt they might be over their heads, Helen remained steadfast in her convictions. She continued her ruse of being a nurse and continued to tell Billy the apartment was part of a hospital. Again and again, she reminded him of what to do if anyone should knock on the apartment door.

"Run to the bathroom and hide in the cabinet," Helen said. "And don't make so much as a peep." Billy always agreed, and for his cooperation, Helen gave him another ether-spiked piece of candy. The more of these he ate, though, the sicker Billy became. He wished she'd stop giving him the awful-tasting things, but he didn't want to disappoint her by saying so.

As if waiting to hear from the kidnappers wasn't difficult enough, Billy's family were deluged with rumors that sprouted daily and spread indiscriminately. On Friday evening, one such rumor appeared so suddenly and gained steam so quickly that, for a moment, even James was hopeful, although he knew better than to share his optimism with Isabella. Half a dozen men swore that they'd seen Billy at Cleveland's Euclid Hotel and that the man with the child had been arrested. Ever the alpha dog, Buhl left for Cleveland immediately only to learn that this, too, was a wild goose chase. Police had detained a boy and man in Cleveland, and even Buhl had to admit the child bore a striking resemblance to Billy. But it was not his nephew.

By noon on Saturday, police received multiple reports that Billy had been spotted in Ashtabula, Ohio, about forty miles north of Warren on the shore of Lake Erie. Perkins men swarmed to the region, and Pennsylvania mounted police stopped all traffic at the state line. It, too, was another dead-end.

Buhl called his brother-in-law to tell him both leads had proven fruitless. Whitla, whose nerves by now had the better of him, collapsed.

Back in Sharon, the post office assigned a special carrier to the Whitla home. Piles of letters arrived each day, many offering the family advice and sympathy. Others, though, were cruelly manipulative. More than one sender

James Boyle would do anything Helen asked. His loyalty earned him a life sentence.

claimed to be the kidnapper. Their ransom notes promised Billy's safe return if various substantial sums were paid. The one saving grace was that the family knew that the real kidnappers made Billy address the envelopes. This, at least, made it easy to separate the cranks from the real criminals.

On Saturday, the Whitlas finally received what they so desperately needed: a letter telling them how to pay the kidnappers' ransom demand of $10,000. It was to be delivered in fives, tens, and twenties—Helen's idea. The drop was to be made in Ashtabula. James Whitla was instructed on what route to travel, presumably indicating he would be followed. He was to go to the Smith Hotel, where another letter was waiting in the name of C. A. White. That letter would offer the final instructions, including where to leave the ransom money.

Also included was a heartbreakingly affectionate letter from Billy. It read:

"Dear Papa: Tell mama not to worry. I will be home with her tomorrow. I am in a house that has many trees around it. I am well now. Your loving son, Billy."

Whitla planned to leave for Ashtabula late Saturday evening. He notified the police departments in the jurisdictions through which he'd travel not to follow him or make a move on the kidnappers. Just as he was heading out, G. B. Perkins arrived at the Whitla home. He refused to allow James to leave before his men recorded the serial numbers on all of the bills in the ransom payment. Whitla was furious and sick with worry that this would interfere with the very clear instructions the kidnappers had given him. His concerns proved justified. The delay caused him to take another train to Ashtabula—a completely different route than the one demanded by the kidnappers. Blind with fear and panic, James plodded onward.

Upon arrival at the Smith Hotel in Ashtabula, the clerk delivered devastating news. There was no such guest of the hotel named C. A. White, so the clerk had taken it upon himself to open the letter. Realizing the subject matter, he called the police. James nearly vomited from terror. The kidnappers would now think he had been the one to betray them.

In sheer desperation, James felt he had only one option. He rushed to Flatiron Park, the site of the original drop, and left the money as he was told. Perhaps he could still satisfy the kidnappers. Perhaps he could still save his son.

Unbeknownst to James, Buhl ordered Perkins detectives to tail his brother-in-law, both for his own safety and to ensure the money made it to the kidnappers. By 4 a.m., with the ransom still untouched, James lost all hope of retrieving Billy. His Perkins shadow, Detective McCain, accompanied the broken man to Cleveland, where Frank Buhl waited. Both Buhl and G. B. Perkins still believed they would find the kidnappers and Billy in this city.

Helen was furious when James returned home without the ransom. She closed the bedroom door, but Billy could hear them arguing.

"What do we do now?" Helen, enraged, shouted at James. "What do we do with him?"

Fortunately for Billy, G. B. Perkins had a plan, and he convinced both Billy's uncle and father to follow it. Somehow, they got a letter published in the *Cleveland Plain Dealer* Sunday paper. It explained that the clerk of the Smith Hotel had been the one to interfere in the ransom plan and that the unforeseen problems were not the fault of James Whitla. They asked for one more opportunity to pay the money and promised that all detectives would be withdrawn from Ohio. The entire party then left Cleveland for Sharon, Pennsylvania, where they awaited a response in the Whitla home.

Isabella let out a cry of relief on Monday when the mail carrier handed her an envelope written in her son's childish, recognizable hand. The kidnappers had seen their letter and were willing to give the family one last chance. James was to return to Cleveland, leave the ransom in a public space, then wait in the Hollenden Hotel.

For the broken James Whitla, that final train ride to Cleveland was pure hell, but he managed to marshal every remaining ounce of strength he had for the journey. He followed the kidnappers' instructions to the letter. First, he got off at Wilson Avenue. Next, he went to Theodore Urban's drugstore at the corner of St. Clair Avenue. A letter retrieved from the drugstore told him to go to a confectioner at the corner of 53rd and Standard Streets. It was here he left the ransom money in a package addressed to Mr. W. P. Hays. James then went to the Hollenden to wait.

It took little time for the hotel patrons to recognize his face and surmise his mission. They waited anxiously with him as he stared at the revolving doors. Dozens of people came and went, blocking the view of the sidewalk. As his panic grew, James's panic grew, and he feared that he had once again failed—that he had let his son down. His breath quickened. His legs weakened. He thought he might pass out. Suddenly, a voice pierced the chatter and hum of the hotel.

"It's him! It's him!"

Reporters, tipped off to James Whitla's presence in the Hollenden, darted to the phones. Photographers rushed toward the shouts. And, miraculously, through the yielding throng, there emerged a dazed little boy dressed in a cap, knickerbocker shorts, and steel-rimmed glasses.

The crowd erupted into an impromptu celebration, but one voice rose above the cacophony.

"Billy!" James screamed.

The ether-impaired child needed several seconds to recognize the man reaching for him. Finally, the penny dropped.

"Daddy!" Billy exclaimed. "I'm so glad I found you!"

Hotel patrons slapped one another on the back, expressing the joy of a nation. "We did it!" they congratulated one another. "Billy's safe."

Soon the hundreds of people now filling the hotel lobby began chanting, "Speech! Speech! Speech!"

An exhausted yet grateful James Whitla told them, "If I lived a thousand years, I would never be able to thank you. I've found my boy." With that, he asked the hotel clerk to connect him with Sharon, Pennsylvania, so he could tell his family that Billy was coming home.

Helen crowed and hugged the ransom money as if it were human. She kissed and congratulated James before she told him how different and adventurous their lives would now be. But, she warned, public sentiment would be against them, so they had to play it cool and pretend nothing had changed.

Worried that some vengeful local might shoot them on sight, Helen convinced her lover that they needed to stay in the apartment for several more days. Once the heat subsided, they could make their break, she said.

The last person Helen thought she needed to fear was Billy. It was a miscalculation she would soon regret. Though she'd done her best to befuddle the child, he had an amazingly accurate memory of the buildings, streets, and trees he'd seen outside the apartment windows, and he described all of it to the police. The delighted Helen wasn't thinking about any of that as she and James plotted their escape with James Whitla's money. In fact, Helen believed she'd planned for every eventuality. She covered her face with a thick veil and carried a basket as if going to the market. She left by the front door, chuckling as she passed several detectives studying the buildings on her block. James left through the basement. The couple met at the grocer's shop. Their plan was to take a train out of Cleveland, but Helen's love of fashion got the best of her.

"Let's stop for drinks," she cooed to James, "and then I'm going to buy a new outfit before we board."

Ever subservient, James suggested O'Reilly's on Ontario Street. O'Reilly was an old friend from Sharon. What harm would it do to have one last drink with an old pal?

Unfortunately for both of them, one drink wasn't enough. A few hours later, Helen was good and drunk. She climbed up on her chair, put one foot on the table, and began her usual pub routine.

"Drink to me!" she shouted to the bar's patrons. "I am an actress and an artist and a money getter."

O'Reilly never knew the plumber Boyle to have as much money as he was throwing at the barkeep. He'd certainly also never seen James Boyle in the company of a woman like this. It was clear the two were celebrating something special. What that was, Boyle wouldn't say, but O'Reilly had his suspicions.

By now, there was no chance of Helen making it to a dress shop, let alone the two of them making it to their train. Boyle asked O'Reilly when the last car left Cleveland. There would be one final train heading to Chicago shortly, O'Reilly told him.

Boyle struggled to get the wild and intoxicated Helen down from her table and out the door onto the street. As soon as he did, O'Reilly called the police.

The stumbling, inebriated couple barely made it four blocks before they were nabbed.

Boyle denied even knowing Helen and thought he was clever when he told police his name was Jones. What he didn't realize was that Billy Whitla had already told them his alias.

Helen fell back on her favorite sobriquet, Helene Falkner. She vacillated between anger, flattery, cajoling, and physically fighting the police. In the end, she failed miserably in her denials of involvement in the kidnapping. The bills taped under her dress were all the evidence police needed.

The couple was sent back to Mercer County, Pennsylvania, to stand trial. Neither took the stand in their own defense—but Billy Whitla testified, and his calm and confident manner delivered the couple a prison sentence. Boyle was given life. Helen was fined $5,000 and sentenced to twenty-four years.

Immediately after the trial, Isabella Whitla was asked to offer her advice on how other parents could keep their children safe.

"Be careful of his friends," she replied. "Never let him go off unattended. And tell him to never accept candy from strangers."

9

IRENE SCHROEDER, THE FIRST WOMAN TO FACE PENNSYLVANIA'S ELECTRIC CHAIR

W hatever else she did or didn't do, one thing is true: Irene Schroeder was a liar. She didn't care about what or to whom she lied; the fact was she said whatever she needed to say to get whatever it was she wanted.

She was tough, but that was no surprise, given her upbringing. The northern panhandle in which her hometown sits is part of the Ohio Valley, a region created by the three bordering states of Pennsylvania, Ohio, and West Virginia. Like its largest city, Wheeling, the surrounding small towns sit at the base of the Appalachian Mountains, nestled along a curve in the Ohio River. The water splits Wheeling into eastern and western halves. In the middle is Wheeling Island, where many wealthy residents built homes in the 1920s and 1930s, when the region enjoyed its best economy and highest population numbers.

Pre-Depression, the people of the Ohio Valley were, in the main, farmers, railroad laborers, millworkers, and miners. They were independently minded hard workers and—unlike Virginia, to which West Virginia originally belonged—vehemently anti-slavery. This sentiment only grew stronger when large numbers of German families, like the Shraders, joined the community.

Irene's first documented lie was the age at which she married Homer Shrader. (That is the actual spelling of her surname; Irene changed it because she thought it would help her escape her life and crimes.) She declared herself twenty-one years of age on the marriage license, probably because that is how old Homer was. But Irene was actually born on February 18, 1909, in Benwood, Marshall County, West Virginia. That means she was only fifteen when she married Homer, three years younger than the legal age of consent. She was even a year too young for the state's exception that allowed minors to marry with parental consent.

Irene's father, Joseph Crawford, was a fish salesman. Her mother, Martha, died when Irene was young. She was forty-seven when her youngest daughter was born. In fact, she had been pregnant for half of her life. Irene was Martha's twelfth child and one of the nine that survived.

There was a four-year age difference between Irene and her brother Tom. They were the youngest of the Crawford children and apparently quite close. Close enough, at least, that Tom was an accomplice in many of Irene's crimes in addition to working his solo career. Their older brother, Edward, was also a career criminal who was killed by the sheriff of Osage County, Missouri, during an attempted prison escape in 1931.

Based on the age of Irene's own son, Donnie, it isn't a great leap to assume that Irene and Homer married because Irene was pregnant. It certainly wasn't a marriage forged from an eternal bond, as her departure with eighteen-month-old Donnie seems to indicate. The couple never divorced, nor was there ever an attempt at reconciliation. They simply constructed separate lives. A short one, in Irene's case.

When Irene ran from Homer, she didn't run far. She moved just three and a half miles up the road to Wheeling, where she found a furnished room and a job as a waitress. Whether she was really as wild as her reputation is anyone's guess, but she had an undeniable propensity for getting attention. A natural entertainer, waitressing was an—albeit poor—substitute for a stage career. The gregarious Irene joked and laughed as she served the cafe's patrons and soon developed her own regular clientele. One man developed a particular fondness for the fleshy, peroxide blond, and he was the last man on earth anyone would suspect of susceptibility to temptation.

Walter Glenn Dague was to boring normalcy what Irene was to unbridled flirtation. Nine years Irene's senior, Glenn (as he was known) seemed to do everything that was expected of a man in the early twentieth century. On June 5, 1917, at the age of twenty-one, the Sunday school teacher registered for the draft for the first World War. He served one year as a private in the 46th Infantry. After the war, he returned home to live with his parents while working in a packing plant. In June 1920, he married Theresa Hess, and the couple had two sons. Glenn presented himself as a deeply religious man—until he ran into Irene. Literally.

By 1927, Glenn was working as a car insurance salesman. One rainy summer day, as he drove along a Wheeling street, a young woman darted out from the sidewalk. Glenn slowed but could not stop his vehicle, and he soundly thumped the girl with his front bumper. She landed in the road, unhurt save for a dirty waitress uniform and torn stockings. How the rest of the tale unraveled depends upon whom you believe.

As Irene told it, Glenn offered to drive her home to change clothes so she could make it back to her waitress shift on time. She fell in love with him right then and there, she told reporters, and bemoaned how different her life might have been had she married Glenn and not Homer. He was the first person in her life, she said, "to believe good about me instead of bad."

Oddly, all of these warm and fuzzy feelings didn't prevent Irene from running off to North Carolina with another man. This relationship was complicated, however, by Irene's giving birth to Glenn's baby, an infant that lived just two days. "It was a trauma," said Irene, that forced her to realize that it was Glenn she truly wanted, and she returned to Wheeling to find him.

Family, friends, and fellow church members were shocked when Glenn abandoned his family for the twenty-year-old, married, single mother. It was the first of many surprising things they'd learn about the Sunday school teacher.

In April 1929, Glenn left his job selling insurance and took a position with the Scott Motor Company, a Chrysler dealership. His career was irrevocably derailed, however, when—after a dispute about how much commission he was owed—he stole two cars to make up for what he believed he was due. Glenn hid the cars on Wheeling Island, then told Irene to pack for Toledo, Ohio, where they would live the idyllic life of a married couple, and Glenn would be a father to four-year-old Donnie. It seems that they had both forgotten to factor in how difficult finding employment might be while on the run from auto theft charges. The two jobs Glenn managed to find in Toledo ended in dismissals. He applied for a third job, but his references were returned with a dismal note attached: "Deserted wife and two children."

Both Irene and Glenn answered ads they found in magazines promising guaranteed success and wealth beyond imagining. These were little more than get-rich-quick schemes involving the sales of washing machines, silk stockings, or other little luxuries. Unsurprisingly, none of these "opportunities" panned out as described.

Irene did her part. She took in laundry and other odd jobs, but in the end, it wasn't enough. The couple was evicted. Their only choice, as Glenn saw it, was to drive one of the stolen vehicles to Pittsburgh, Pennsylvania, where Glenn found a job as a ditchdigger and Irene once again worked as a washerwoman. As it turned out, though, Glenn's unemployment curse followed them to the Keystone State. By the summer of 1929, he again found himself without an income. Somehow, he managed to find one last job as an assistant to a tree surgeon, a position for which he was utterly and dangerously unprepared. On one call, he fell out of a tree. Irene nursed him for days until he was able to get back on his feet. It was then, said Irene, that he made his Scarlet O'Hara-esque promise.

"If I can't make an honest living," Walter Glenn Dague declared, "I'll do it another way."

That was Irene's version of the story of how their life of crime began. There is also, however, a contradictory tale, one a bit less made-for-TV. Both stories begin the same, with Glenn nearly running Irene down in the streets of Wheeling, but that is where the similarities ended.

For one thing, Glenn didn't take Irene home to clean herself up for her waitress shift at the cafe. He took her to a seedy hotel in Ohio, where they spent the night. And, if his conversations with *New Castle News* reporter Bart Richards are to be believed, it was the crossing of state lines that sealed

Irene Schroeder's death certificate lists the cause of death as judicial execution. She was the first woman to be electrocuted by the Commonwealth of Pennsylvania.

Glenn's fate. This violated a law known as the Mann Act. Passed in 1910, the law, also known as the White-Slave Traffic Act, made it a felony to transport a woman or girl across state lines for the purposes of immoral activity. This rather vague language gave law enforcement a wide berth to prosecute even those engaging in consensual acts.

While Glenn might not have understood the possible consequences of the tryst, according to reporter Richards's account, Irene most definitely did. She used the threat of the Mann Act to extort money from Glenn. It was only when relatives and friends refused to offer further financial assistance that Glenn agreed to accompany Irene on her bandit escapades.

As the old cliche goes, though, there are three sides to every story: his side, her side, and the truth. The truth was that Glenn was a car thief long before Irene ever had a chance to corrupt him.

Upon arrival in Pittsburgh, they searched for easy targets. Their first choice was a gas station on an isolated road just south of the city. According to a biography of Irene published by the *Youngstown Vindicator*, the pair decided that, like all robbers worth their salt, they needed guns. In August 1929, they purchased two cheap, used pistols from a hardware store. If it was unusual for couples to shop for matching guns, the store owner never mentioned it. Instead, he sold them two weapons, meanwhile cautioning that they weren't representative of his best stock. Ignoring the warning, Irene and Glenn left with their purchase, enthusiastically launching their life of crime.

The first thing the amateur crooks learned about robbing gas stations was that, in most cases, it really didn't matter whether or not your gun actually worked. As soon as the man or woman behind the cash register saw a weapon, they usually threw up their hands and freely offered the till. This being the case, Irene and Glenn must have presumed the bandit life would be a breeze. Just in case, though, after getting safely away from the scene of their first robbery, they decided they should probably test the guns, just in case.

Glenn tried his weapon first. He pointed the barrel at a tree trunk and pulled the trigger. Nothing happened.

Irene's gun actually fired but only once.

Both were lucky the worn-out chunks of scrap metal hadn't exploded in their hands.

Obviously, they needed new guns, but there was a small problem. The gas station robbery had only yielded eleven dollars. So, Irene and Glenn returned to the same Pittsburgh hardware store and bought another set of cheap, used pistols, likely no better than the first two.

For the next four months, the pair committed a string of robberies in West Virginia, Ohio, and western Pennsylvania. The Pittsburgh region was a particular favorite, probably because it was a rural area and, in most cases, had a minimal police presence.

Investigators estimated they were knocking over stores and gas stations at a rate of one per week. In some instances, innocent suspects were jailed and convicted for heists Irene and Glenn actually committed. One West Virginia man, Frank Howell, received a fifteen-year sentence. Fortunately, the duo eventually confessed to the holdup, and Howell was released after fourteen months.

There was one other innocent forced to suffer from these crimes: Irene's son, Donnie, who was seated in the car beside his mother for nearly every robbery. Irene insisted that the two remain together, even though there was a very real possibility he could be hurt or killed as a result of her actions. He'd even taken to calling Glenn "Papa." Also along for many of the thefts was Irene's youngest brother, Tom, who often acted as a lookout during the holdups.

By December 1929, Irene was feeling homesick. She decided to spend Christmas at one of her sister's homes in West Virginia. The respite was short, though, and the next day, they were back on the road to Pennsylvania. On December 27, the gang, including Tom, whether by premeditation or spur-of-the-moment impulse, chose as their target a P. H. Butler grocery store near the Pittsburgh suburb of Butler.

At about 11:45 a.m., while Donnie waited in the car and Tom stood guard outside, Irene and Glenn entered the store, guns drawn. They forced store manager Wish Angert into the stockroom, where they bound his hands, feet, and mouth. After liberating his wallet from his pants pocket, Irene went to the cash register and emptied that as well. They sped northward on the Butler-New Castle Highway (today's Route 422) toward New Castle, their goal to reach and cross the Ohio state line. Unfortunately for the gang, Angert was found and untied by a customer and called the police within moments of the robbery. Irene, Glenn, and Tom had far less of a head start than they thought they did.

At the time of the robbery, there was no physical substation for the Pennsylvania State Police and Pennsylvania Highway Patrol working out of New Castle. Instead, both sets of officers worked out of the Colonial Hotel on East Washington Street. Situated on the hotel's third floor, the office sat midway between the hotel rooms that served as residence barracks. It was a

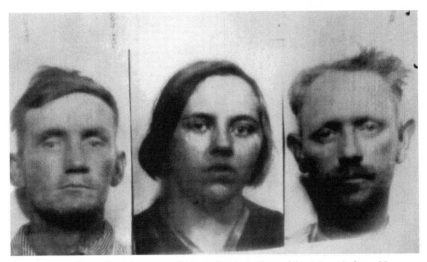

This rare trio of mugshots (courtesy of Alcuin Books in Scottsdale, Arizona) shows Vernon Ackerman, Irene Schroeder, and Walter Glenn Dague.

welcoming home for the police officers stationed there. Hotel owners John and Mollie Crowl were affectionately possessive of the men whom Molly called her boys.

When word of the P. H. Butler holdup came into the Colonial Hotel substation, the state police officers were out on other calls. The only personnel available were highway patrol officers whose only job it was to enforce traffic laws. (These two divisions would merge several years later.) Twenty-four-year-old Corporal Brady Paul took the call and was told that the robbers were likely heading toward New Castle. Paul told fellow highway patrolman Private Ernest Moore to hop in the sidecar, and together they drove several miles out on the Butler-New Castle Highway, where they set up a roadblock near a farm owned by the Baldwin family. They stopped several cars, asked for licenses, and sent the drivers on their way. Paul knew they were specifically seeking a car carrying two men and a woman and could, therefore, easily eliminate the vehicles that didn't meet that description. During lulls in traffic, the two young men passed the time with good-natured snowball fights. It wasn't long before they noticed a green Chevy cresting the hill, heading in their direction.

Paul immediately realized the passengers matched the details he'd been provided. One man was driving, and there was a woman on the passenger side. A second man sat in the rear seat. He hadn't planned to see a little boy standing on the seat in between the two adults, but he nonetheless stopped the vehicle and asked the driver for his license. This is the only fact that all parties agree upon. What happened next depended upon who was telling the story.

According to witness Eva Baldwin, who viewed the incident from inside her home, the driver of the car exited the vehicle as soon as Paul stopped it. A woman got out and stood directly behind him. She then shoved the driver to the side, rammed the barrel of the gun into Paul's stomach, walked him backward toward a telephone pole, and pulled the trigger.

Moore, who had been at the rear of the vehicle recording the license plate, moved toward the front of the car when he heard gunfire. A man in the back seat of the vehicle fired on him through the front windshield. Amazingly, while both bullets found their mark, neither was fatal. One clipped the tip of his nose. The other creased the side of Moore's skull, knocking him unconscious.

Fifteen-year-old witness Howard Ziegler had a slightly different recollection. He said it was a man who first shot at Corporal Brady and that Brady tried to take cover behind the telephone pole as the assailant continued firing.

Leal Baldwin, Eva's nephew, was just twelve when he witnessed the shooting from several yards away. Decades later, at age eighty-three, he shared his memories of the day with a local police historian and newspaper reporter. Leal described seeing the motorcycle park in his aunt's driveway. He watched the two officers' snowball fight. He saw the shots fired at Private Moore through the front windshield. According to Leal, though, Brady Paul was shot in the chest as he approached the driver's window. Paul managed to take cover behind the telephone pole and, though injured multiple times, continued to fire back at the gang. Leal also watched as two men exited the vehicle to move Moore out of the way of the vehicle before they sped off.

Even Ernest Moore's story changed. Many years after the incident, there was talk that he'd confessed that one of his wildly fired shots might have inadvertently struck Corporal Paul, an unfortunate instance of friendly fire.

Glenn eventually admitted that he and Irene had been involved in the New Castle shootout, but his story offered yet another twist. After six hours of questioning by the police, Glenn claimed that officers Paul and Moore did stop the car and that Paul asked for his license. Glenn gave Paul his wallet, and Paul handed it back. For reasons Glenn didn't explain, he then stepped out of the car and drew his gun on the highway patrol officer. Irene exited the car behind him, drawing her pistol as well.

Moore, said Glenn, thrust his hands in the air and took cover behind the vehicle. Paul opened fire and, according to Glenn, either Irene or Tom returned his volleys.

The situation descended into mayhem. "Shots were fired all around me," Glenn said. "One went through my hat, and one grazed my hip."

In keeping with other witness statements, Glenn agreed that Tom fired shots at Private Moore from the back seat and through the front windshield. Glenn also described having to push Moore away from the front of the vehicle so they could get away. Paul, however, was supposedly still firing from behind the telephone pole as the gang raced away.

Regardless of whose bullets struck Paul, the injuries proved fatal. Corporal Brady Paul died in Jameson Memorial Hospital as a result of wounds suffered in the gun battle. In that instant, Irene, Glenn, and Tom graduated from robbers to murderers. Pennsylvania law, then and now, states that anyone involved in a robbery in which a murder occurs is guilty of that murder, whether he or she actually pulls the trigger or not. The manhunt for the murderers of Brady Paul had officially begun.

Irene was smart enough to know that the green Chevy needed to go. In New Castle, the trio traveled side streets looking for a suitable replacement. Ray C. Horton and his passenger, Elsie Mickum, provided a convenient target, and Irene and the men hijacked their Chrysler at gunpoint. It was flashier than Irene would have liked, but the bright-blue sedan with shiny aluminum wheels got them out of Pennsylvania and into Ohio. From there, they sped to Wheeling, West Virginia, where they stashed the Chrysler and dropped Tom. His whereabouts would baffle the police for several years to come.

Before she and Glenn slipped away in one of Glenn's stolen vehicles, Irene made one final arrangement. She left Donnie in the safe care of her father in nearby Benwood.

While Irene and Dague might have been able to outrun local police, they couldn't outrun the technology of the day. It wasn't just newswires carrying the gang's description; the police were using their own new high-tech communications tool as well. Shortly before the shooting, Pennsylvania unveiled its new "telegraph typewriter" system, which connected ninety-five cities and towns across the state. It made sharing of wanted bulletins nearly instantaneous. The problem was, the only details these bulletins could provide were the barest descriptions of the suspects. Telling officers to be on the lookout for a blond woman traveling with two men didn't give them much to go on. These generic details did result in a flood of tips from the general public, most of which were false accusations against innocent people. In one instance, a Salem, Ohio, woman was nearly arrested because she had gone out of town with her husband and five-year-old son—something her neighbors found suspicious.

In the end, it was old-fashioned police work that yielded the first significant break in the case. The initial search of the green Chevy revealed a child's suit of clothing. This corroborated Private Moore's sighting of a young boy in the front seat of the car he and Corporal Brady Paul had stopped. When Pennsylvania State Police Officer Jimmy Brooks and New Castle County Sheriff Harrison "Buck" Reynolds made a second inspection of the vehicle, however, they found a small, handwritten receipt from a store in Wheeling, West Virginia, that the first investigators missed. It listed one item: a red scarf. There was a date and amount on the receipt but no customer name.

Brooks took the ninety-mile trip to the Wheeling store, where he spoke with the chatty salesclerk who had sold the scarf. Not only was she talkative, but she also had a great memory and personally knew the customer who had made the purchase. It was Irene Schroeder from nearby Bellaire, Ohio, she told Brooks.

On December 31, 1929, Pennsylvania police visited the Bellaire home of Irene's sister, Ruby Shrader, wife of Homer's brother, Ray. Also at the Shrader home was Irene's father, Joseph Crawford, and her son, Donnie. Joseph explained to the police that Irene had gone away with her boyfriend several days previously. She had left her son, Donnie, in his care. Joseph, in turn, had taken the boy to Ruby's house.

As the adults spoke, Donnie watched and listened. According to the officers involved in the interview, the sight of their uniforms sparked a spontaneous admission from the boy. "My mommy shot a cop like you," he announced. To illustrate his point, he purportedly added sound effects.

"Boom, boom!" Donnie shouted.

Recognizing the significance of this statement—and likely violating numerous laws—the police officers removed Donnie from his family's care and took the four-year-old boy back across the Ohio state line to Pennsylvania, where he was placed in a juvenile detention home operated by former county detective Jack Dunlap. There, he was held under heavy guard, should Irene or her accomplices come looking for him.

Various versions of Donnie's statement were published in newspapers who now began to fixate on his mother. Interestingly, early coverage of Irene was less than flattering. Her dyed hair was a point of constant discussion, as was the fact that she was "heavyset," a "big blond," and was "round faced." Many reports inaccurately listed her age at thirty or described her as a divorcee. Either way, reports that she'd left her husband for her criminal cohort allowed readers to draw their own juicy conclusions. To hammer home her moral shortcomings, most reporters also added that Glenn had left his wife and children for Irene.

Like Irene's, Brady Paul's legacy was being shaped in the press as well. Certainly, his bravery in facing down the wanton gang featured heavily in news stories, but another element had been introduced to his murder, and that was martyrdom. Paul, reporters claimed, died in large part because he was too gallant to fire on a woman.

Perhaps the most questionable journalistic tactic, though, was using Donnie as bait to keep readers buying newspapers. Even when there were few new details to plaster across front pages, editors could always run photos of handsome little Donnie, son of the murderess blond bandit. In one picture, he sat awkwardly in the lap of a sheriff who beamed a smile toward the camera. In another, he posed with a dog. Like the police who whisked him away from the protection of his family, reporters were simply using Donnie as a convenient tool. Strangely, though, for as important as Donnie's "confession" was, newly elected Lawrence County District Attorney John Powers announced that the boy would not be called to testify if Irene were caught. "I will not ask an innocent child to take the stand," he said, "and possibly send his mother to the electric chair."

As word of the killing of the highway patrolman spread, a reward for the capture of the murderers grew. By January 1, 1930, it reached $3,200—a relative value of about $40,000 in today's money. While dozens of strangers tried to collect the bounty, Irene's family had no interest in helping officers or claiming any part of it. In fact, the only way police collected any information from Irene's relatives was to question them for hours on end until, out of either desperation or exhaustion, they revealed some detail that won their release. Such was the case with Irene's brother, John, who, after six hours, shared the fact that Irene admitted to being part of the shootout with Paul and Moore—a seemingly worthless tip since the police already knew this.

On January 3, a sketch made by a Wheeling artist for whom Irene once posed was shown to Donnie. He identified her from the drawing and also confirmed Glenn's identity from a photograph. Meanwhile, the blue sedan used in the couple's escape from Pennsylvania was found in the Wheeling Island garage Glenn used to hide his thefts. Additionally, police arrested friends who had been boarding in the same Pittsburgh rooming house as Irene and Glenn, initially assuming they had taken part in the robbery spree.

Days later, a woman thought to be Irene was arrested and taken to a Youngstown, Ohio, prison. Ray Horton and Elsie Nickum traveled there in the hopes of identifying her as the thief who hijacked their car. They were disappointed to see that the police had the wrong woman.

Newspaper readers woke up on January 8 to see the first published photograph of Irene. In it, she looked young, perhaps high school age, her smile easy and unforced. Soon after, the press ran a photo of Glenn. There was no longer any question about what the couple looked like. The stakes for Irene and Glenn became significantly higher.

Irene and Glenn continued to rob gas stations and stores to fund their trip west. After dropping off Donnie at his grandfather's house, the pair drove one hundred miles south to Parkersburg, West Virginia, where they once again switched cars and retrieved clothing and other supplies left by friends they never named. It was at this point that Irene began dressing like a boy to further obscure her identity.

From West Virginia, Irene and Glenn crossed into bordering Kentucky, then Missouri after that. It was here, after more than a week on the run, that they met their first resistance. A sharp-eyed St. Louis police officer recognized the couple from the photos that had now been distributed nationwide. The officer drew his gun on Glenn, and the two exchanged fire. Luckily, unlike Paul, this officer escaped unscathed. According to Irene, however, Paul was shot in the shoulder. It was at this point that Irene emerged from the car brandishing her own gun. She charged toward the cop and managed to seize his weapon. When the officer whistled for backup from fellow patrolmen, the couple fled, once again evading arrest.

After Missouri, they dropped down to a more southerly route to their ultimate destination, the West Coast. Glenn had heard there were plenty of jobs in the lettuce fields in California. He convinced Irene they could start over there and escape all of the havoc they'd left behind in Pennsylvania. He was right about the employment opportunities. In 1930, California was producing half of the lettuce grown in the United States. (Today, it's closer to 75 percent.) It's hard to imagine, though, how living on a farmhand's salary might have satisfied Irene.

The duo eventually reached Arizona. To confuse anyone looking for a man and woman, Irene and Glenn picked up hitchhikers as they traveled. One passenger, according to Irene, traveled nearly 250 miles with them. When he reached his destination, he filled their gas tank and gave them whatever change he had in his pockets. In Arizona, they stopped for a man limping along the side of the road, his foot wrapped in what appeared to be a bloody bandage. He gave his name as Joe Wells and told them he'd just been released from Oklahoma State Penitentiary. Joe was not averse to deception as Irene suspected when she took a closer look at the "bandage." It was nothing more than an old rag dotted with ketchup. Nonetheless, Joe seemed to fit in well with the merry band of bandits, and he remained in their company until all three reached the point of no return.

The fugitives and their hitchhiker made a stop in the small town of Florence, Arizona. Perhaps they simply needed gasoline. More likely, Glenn and Joe—who entered the store while Irene waited in the car—planned to rob the place. Whatever the truth, while Irene sat in the vehicle, a deputy sheriff named Joe Chapman happened upon the scene. It felt suspicious. He asked Irene for identification.

Irene blew the car horn. To the deputy's surprise, two men ran from the store, tackled him, and threw him inside the running vehicle.

According to reporter Bart Richards's recollections, Glenn demanded that the sheriff show them the way to California. Suspecting that he wouldn't live to reach the final destination, the wily Chapman took the criminals on a back-road wild goose chase that ended up right back in Chandler, where they'd started.

Numerous witnesses to Chapman's kidnapping had alerted the police to the incident and offered descriptions of the car in which he'd been taken. When Glenn drove into Chandler, he was met by three officers with guns drawn.

Glenn gunned the engine. As they drove past the posse, someone—probably Joe Wells—chucked Deputy Sheriff Chapman out of the speeding vehicle. Deputy Sheriff Lee Wright opened fire. Irene returned the fire. She clipped Wright in the shoulder, unwittingly puncturing an artery.

The trio sped west until they reached the Gila River at the foot of the Estrella Mountains. Much of the range—then and now—belongs to the Gila River Indian Reservation. Petroglyphs appear throughout the rock outcroppings, created by the native peoples that have inhabited the rough and rocky land for millennia. Amazingly, it would be descendants of these native peoples who would finally capture "Iron Irene," her lover, and the hapless hitchhiker who simply came along for the ride.

Whether they ran out of gas or simply thought it would be easier to hide or escape into the mountains, the outlaws abandoned their car near Laveen and waded across the Gila River. One version of the story says that Glenn and Joe carried Irene across the water to prevent her from being swept away. Another, more cinema-esque account says the three tore their clothing into strips so that the men could swing Irene across the fast-moving water.

Regardless of the creativity of their methods of absconding, a posse was, by now, tracking the outlaws. It was a diverse crew that included law enforcement, average citizens, ranchers, men from the Gila River Indian Community, and Piipaash (or Pee-Posh) tribe member Leon Sundust, a local "Indian Rodeo" hero and a member of the Maricopa Indian Community. An airplane circled overhead in the clear, sunlit sky as searchers on horseback, in automobiles, and on foot joined the chase.

As the posse closed in, the bandit trio took cover behind a huge rock, the size of a city bus, and began firing on their would-be captors.

Based on his horse-handling skills and lifelong knowledge of the area—Laveen was his hometown—Sundust devised a plan. He and another man, Deputy Jack Carter, broke away from the main posse and picked their way out around the position Irene, Glenn, and Joe had established. Sundust then continued northward before turning around and approaching the outlaws from the higher ground behind them. All the while, rock chips rained down from the hill as bullets from the bandits, the posse, and the airplane overhead ricocheted off boulders and crags. With ammunition running low, the unexpected appearance of Sundust and Carter convinced the fugitives that giving up was better than dying in the rugged Arizona mountain range.

The January 14, 1930, capture of "trigger woman" Irene Schroeder and her lover Glenn Dague created even more salacious headlines than had the original murder and flight, but the press's attitudes were changing. Where Irene had once been dismissed as an overweight, peroxide-haired mother, she was now a "pretty blond woman." Glenn Dague, never a man anyone might describe as handsome, had transformed into Irene's "dapper paramour." Regardless of how they were portrayed or why they were popular fodder for newspaper editors, Irene enjoyed the attention. Even immediately after her surrender in the Estrella Mountains, as she was taken away by a deputy sheriff on horseback, she gazed directly at a photographer capturing the moment and flashed an expression that simultaneously conveyed both defiance and pleasure.

Initially, Irene refused to divulge her real name. She insisted she was not the gun-toting, cop-murdering Irene Schroeder but rather Mildred Winthrop. Glenn, she claimed, was her husband, Albert Winthrop. But unlike Irene, who seemed to bask in the drama of their arrest, Glenn was quiet and more cooperative. He was the only one of the three to admit his true identity.

Meanwhile, the hitchhiker was playing his own what's-my-name gambit. It didn't take long, though, to establish that the stranger who blindly followed Irene and Glenn into a shootout with a seventy-five-man posse was not Joe Wells but rather Vernon Ackerman, son to a good, albeit disappointed, family in Pittsburgh. It was a tremendous letdown to the Pennsylvania State Police, who, until that moment, assumed this second man to be Irene's brother, Tom Crawford.

All three were arraigned the same day they were arrested. Irene appeared before Judge Clarence E. Ice in a stylish blue ensemble donated by an unidentified woman from Phoenix. Bail was set at $15,000 each, and the next hearing was scheduled for January 23. By then, authorities expected receipt of photos and fingerprints airmailed to Phoenix from Harrisburg from which official identification could be made. Lawrence County officials, however, had no interest in seeing the couple tried out of state. A police officer had been killed in their jurisdiction, and the county district attorney was anxious to bring Irene and Glenn back and try them for murder. As Irene attempted to distract with ruses and Glenn sullenly accepted the inevitable, Lawrence County detective H. Martin Lee delivered extradition papers to Harrisburg, where they were signed by Pennsylvania Governor John Stuchell Fisher.

Whether or not Irene and Glenn understood their legal rights or the jeopardy they faced is not certain. Maricopa County Sheriff Charles Wright initially refused to allow either to meet or consult with counsel, saying, according to a lurid account in *True Detective* magazine, "That isn't the method of dealing with criminals out here." This refusal of counsel was, as surprising as it might sound, perfectly legal at the time. While the Sixth

Amendment to the Constitution provided a right to counsel for those charged in federal prosecutions, no such right was extended to prisoners charged with felonies at the state level, nor would there be until 1963.

Regardless of their lack of legal advice or acumen, common sense told the pair that kidnapping and assault would carry a lesser penalty than murder. On January 18, in an attempt to escape extradition back to Pennsylvania, they confessed to kidnapping Deputy Chapman and assaulting him with intent to murder. Prosecuting attorney George T. Wilson assailed the tactic as a ploy to avoid answering for their killing of Corporal Brady Paul. Arizona Superior Court Judge Marlin T. Phelps agreed with Wilson and rejected the plea.

While Irene was wrangling with the Arizona courts, her father was fighting in Pennsylvania for the return of his grandson. Donnie, Joseph Crawford argued, was removed from his home illegally and coerced into giving the damning statement about his mother's involvement in the shooting. Funded by donations from neighbors, friends, and strangers, Joseph hired attorney Benjamin Rosenbloom who filed a writ of habeas corpus—in short, a demand that authorities "produce the body" of the child and prove why they had any right to detain him. In response, the Lawrence County district attorney named the child a material witness and placed him under a $20,000 bond. Joseph was forced to end his fight.

On January 22, Irene and Glenn asked for a twenty-four-hour continuance on the extradition to collect evidence that proved they weren't in Pennsylvania on December 27, 1929. Their request was denied by Arizona Governor John Calhoun Phillips, who knew something the pair likely did not: Pennsylvania's extradition party was already on its way. The hearing briefly recessed, and when the judge returned to his bench, the defendants surprised all parties by announcing they would willingly accept removal to Pennsylvania.

The group assigned to escort Irene and Glenn back to the Keystone State was both sizable and sundry. Lawrence County was well represented, having sent its county detective H. Martin "Peck" Lee, Sheriff Frank Johnston, witness Clarence Evans, and New Castle jail matron Minnie McKibbon. The Pennsylvania State Police contingent included Lieutenant Tom

Boetner, Sargent Edward Bergen, and, of course, Private Ernest Moore. Also invited to join the extradition party was reporter Bart Richards.

The inclusion of a woman was of special delight to those following the case, and Minnie McKibbon was perfectly cast for the role. Before taking the job of jail matron, she'd served as Mercer County deputy sheriff under her father, Sheriff William Riddle. Minnie confidently announced that she would be carrying a gun while fulfilling her duty as immediate caretaker of Irene, as she would with any other prisoner.

"I always go armed," Minnie explained, "but usually I can appeal to women prisoners to be reasonable so there is no need for a weapon."

She would come to rue this confidence when called to testify at trial.

The train ride to Arizona was long and uncomfortable. The group left New Castle for Cleveland, where they boarded the New York Central to Chicago. From Illinois, they made the nearly eight-hour journey to Tucumcari, New Mexico, on the Rock Island Railroad before boarding the Southern Pacific to Phoenix. They could have driven to Phoenix on Route 66, completed only a few years earlier, but—for transporting prisoners—train travel was the more cost-effective, convenient, and secure option.

Upon the party's arrival in Arizona, they presented Governor Phillips with extradition papers for Irene and Glenn, which he immediately signed. He also signed warrants for the arrests of Irene, Glenn, and Thomas Crawford, whom they still suspected Ackerman to be. Within moments, Irene and Glenn were taken to an undisclosed location to await the trip back to Pennsylvania. Though Ackerman would remain there on his own charges, Arizona authorities were happy to see the fugitives from Pennsylvania leave. At the time, Deputy Lee Wright, who was injured during the Chandler shootout, was still in the hospital but expected to recover, so it seemed easier to have someone else deal with the trouble and expense of their trials. It would be but a matter of days before the governor regretted his somewhat hasty decision.

There was no rest for the Pennsylvania extradition team. They reboarded the train for their journey back to New Castle on the same day they arrived. The nearer to Lawrence County they drew, the larger the crowds that greeted them. In Warren, Ohio (forty-one miles west of New Castle), a substantial crowd gathered. It, in turn, was dwarfed by the crowd in Niles, which was itself paltry when compared to the supposed 10,000 people waiting on the platform in Youngstown. When the train finally arrived in the more sparsely populated Pennsylvania county of Lawrence, it was met with an astonishing 3,500 spectators. Twelve special railroad officers were assigned to handle crowd control.

The removal of the prisoners from the train was carefully orchestrated. When Glenn deboarded, he was handcuffed to only one man, County Detective Peck Lee. Irene, by contrast, was handcuffed between two men: Lieutenant Boetner of the state police and Lawrence County Sheriff Frank Johnston. The implications were clear. Firstly, both branches of law enforcement were taking credit for her capture. Secondly, the show of force sent a message to onlookers, press photographers, and, of course, the potential jury pool that Irene Schroeder—"golden tiger," "gun girl," "blonde bandit"—was a dangerous, conniving killer.

Like Charles Wright in Arizona, Lawrence County Sheriff Johnston refused to allow visits from either Donnie or Irene and Glenn's attorneys, but that didn't seem to diminish Irene's fine mood. She joked, sang songs of the day, enjoyed gifts of candy, and generally seemed to enjoy her time in jail. She was regularly visited by two of her sisters, who also visited Donnie at the juvenile detention center. Glenn, on the other hand, spent his days in solitude and kept his thoughts and emotions to himself.

It took some time, but Irene's sisters were eventually successful in hiring Youngstown lawyer K. H. Powell to represent her. The sisters made it quite clear, however, that Irene was his *sole* client, still leaving Glenn without counsel.

Over the next several days, Irene's defense team grew to include William P. Barnum, a former Ohio judge, Oscar Stevens, Thomas Dickey, and former Pennsylvania state senator Benjamin Jarrett. The number of attorneys seemed compatible with the number of criminal charges she faced. These included the murder of Corporal Brady Paul in Pennsylvania, assault with deadly intent on Paul's fellow officer Private Ernest Moore, a shooting and bank robbery in Texas, the kidnapping of Deputy Sheriff Joe Chapman in Arizona, the shooting of Arizona Deputy Sheriff Lee Wright, armed assault in Missouri, and a prodigious string of gas station and grocery store holdups in Pennsylvania. One publication described Irene's menu of crimes as "more charges than any woman in history."

On January 27, attorney Powell was finally permitted to visit Irene in her cell. As he left the jail, he revealed to reporters that Irene was not in the best of health. An operation for appendicitis performed two years earlier, he explained, had never healed properly, leaving Irene in near-constant pain. An alternate version of events had Irene fainting while receiving a visit from her little son, Donnie, still a resident of the county's juvenile detention center. Neither story garnered much traction or sympathy, but Irene's defense attorney would soon face a far more ominous challenge than her widely disregarded illnesses. On January 29, Maricopa County Deputy Sheriff Lee Wright died in a Mesa, Arizona, hospital from wounds received in his gun battle with Irene and Glenn. An angry Governor Phillips demanded that the killers be brought back to Arizona.

When told about Wright's death, both Irene and Glenn offered comment. "That is too bad," Irene said, "but we didn't shoot him."

Glenn further explained that Wright "was shot by someone in the posse."

Regardless of these denials, the couple's rap sheet was now augmented by yet another charge of first-degree murder.

Whether Irene truly cared for Glenn or simply wanted control of his defense, she refused to continue on as a client of K. H. Powell et al. unless they agreed to also represent her lover. Two days after receiving word of Lee Wright's death, Thomas Dickey made his first visit to W. Glenn Dague's cell in the New Castle jail. Dickey was likely Glenn's first visitor as his family had deserted him when his infamous crimes became public. The money for Glenn's defense likely came from the funds volunteered to Irene, as he had no resources of his own.

As it turned out, Irene and Glenn weren't the only ones employing high-powered lawyers. Brady Paul's family had recruited Frank S. Ruff of nearby Jeannette, Pennsylvania, to assist the prosecutors. Ruff respectfully bowed out, however, when legal legend Charles J. Margiotti was named special prosecutor by Pennsylvania Attorney General Cyrus E. Woods. (Margiotti himself would serve in that capacity in 1935 and again in 1950.)

The January 31 preliminary hearing was perfunctorily brief. The prosecution called a handful of witnesses; the defense called none. Thomas Dickey believed that witnesses would only tip his hand as to their defense strategy. In a ruling that surprised no one, Irene and Glenn were held without bail. A grand jury would convene on March 3, 1930, to determine on which crimes, if any, the pair would be indicted.

During the weeks between the arraignment and the impaneling of the grand jury, the public's interest in how Irene behaved in prison was insatiable. They wanted the scoop on how she ate (well, according to Sheriff Johnston), what she read, who visited her, and how she spent her hours in captivity. Irene, said Johnston and his wife, turned to religion to fill her time. This sudden interest felt a bit contrived to some observers. Unlike Glenn, who had a lifelong affiliation with the church, Irene's newfound faith seemed arbitrary. Nonetheless, she ardently read the Bible and sang hymns that Glenn could hear from his cell.

While Irene and Glenn adapted to jail life, their attorneys confronted several pressing legal issues. The Cleveland police believed the duo might have been responsible for the shooting of an officer several months previously. An Ohio ballistics expert arrived in New Castle on February 4, and although he refused to comment on his activities, it was assumed he was seeking a connection between the bullets collected from Irene and Glenn and those used on the Cleveland patrolman. The allegation eventually proved false.

The more important decision to make was whether or not the partners in crime should be tried together or separately. And should the trial even be held in New Castle, or was it advisable to ask for a change of venue? On top of these concerns, Arizona Governor Phillips was growing more impatient. Whether it was a fact or just a ploy to stave off Phillips's efforts to take Irene and Glenn back west, Sheriff Johnston and County Detective Peck Lee revealed a conversation that seemed to bolster Glenn's version of events. When in Arizona as part of the extradition team, the two men said, Sheriff Charles Wright had admitted to them that Lee Wright was shot by fellow officers—not Irene and Glenn. The only way to break the resulting impasse was a compromise. If the prosecutors in Lawrence County sought the death penalty, Phillips would forego extradition efforts.

The twosome was now facing the electric chair. If found guilty, Irene would be the first woman in Pennsylvania to be executed by electrocution.

Glenn's family learned early on that the best way to stay out of the limelight was to avoid any relationship with Glenn, an approach that, for the most part, worked. Irene's family couldn't seem to escape her notoriety. Her son, father, sisters, brothers-in-law, and estranged husband were all objects of press coverage and speculation. Even distant relatives like Ralph W. Holland couldn't avoid the Schroeder stigma. When sentenced to seven years in the West Virginia State Penitentiary for burglary, Holland was identified as "Irene's cousin." When Irene's brother John was arraigned in Wheeling for driving while intoxicated, she figured prominently in the news stories. For her family, there was simply no way to dodge this truth: sharing blood with Irene cast a shade of infamy on all of them.

On February 17, 1930, Irene had the dubious honor of turning twenty-one in jail. Regardless of the sentiment of the citizenry, her father and several other family members visited. It was a tense celebration at best. Two days later, a strange rumor appeared and proliferated, one Lawrence County officials had to aggressively tamp down. The buzz was that Irene had escaped from jail, her whereabouts unknown. Where the rumor was born or how it spread so quickly, no one knew. Its very existence, however, illustrated the level of interest in the case and the community's overwhelming belief that Irene was a terrifying, near-supernatural threat.

Irene did have her supporters. Most, like the women's groups that demanded she be tried in private, didn't necessarily believe she was innocent—they simply didn't want to see her put to death. This decision was out of their hands, of course, and when the grand jury convened on March 3, 1930, it indicted the couple on charges of murder, manslaughter, assault and battery with the intent to kill, and highway robbery.

Irene and Glenn would be tried separately, with the prosecuting attorneys making the choice of who went first. They chose Irene.

Seven days later, the process of seating a jury began. It took three days and five panels of sixty potential jurors each for ten men and two women to finally be installed in the jury box near presiding Judge R. Lawrence Hildebrand.

It's highly unlikely that anyone thought Irene would be acquitted of the multitude of charges for which she stood trial. Even her attorneys announced that their singular goal was to keep Irene out of the electric chair. Between her own admissions and the dozens of eyewitnesses called by the prosecution, it was clear that much of Irene's short life had been spent perpetrating one kind of transgression or another. Still, the case was followed with avid interest as one fascinating character after another paraded past through the courthouse doors.

Mattie Jackson, an alleged narcotics user, was one of Irene's cellmates in Arizona. She testified that Irene confessed to the killing of Brady Paul in Pennsylvania. Sheriff Charles Wright assured the New Castle jury that he did not allow newspapers in his prison, implying that Mattie could only know the details to which she testified through conversations with Irene.

Petty thief Rose Smith, another of Irene's Arizona cellmates, relayed Irene's stories of fleeing Pennsylvania and the shootout with the St. Louis police.

Jail matron Martha McKibbon testified that Irene smiled after learning how many bullets had pierced Corporal Brady Paul. In a more uncomfortable exchange, McKibbon also admitted the shoulder holster for her celebrated side pistol had been taken some time during her matron duties. She thought the culprit might have been Irene.

Though extensive, not all of the prosecution's evidence was unimpeachable, nor were there a lack of mistakes by law enforcement. Bullets were entered into evidence that were purportedly found on sidewalks or under automobile seats, but most were neither marked at the time of collection nor documented prior to trial. They were simply entered in the record on the word of witnesses. Reporter Bart Richards testified that he had been given one of the bullets from the Pennsylvania shootout as a souvenir. He subsequently lost it when the suit that he'd been wearing when he received it was sent to the dry cleaner. These deficiencies were counterbalanced by ballistics expert Louis Marr, who was far less famous and respected than the legendary forensics expert Calvin Goddard for whom he worked. Nonetheless, in the eyes of journalists and, presumably, the jury, his testimony was burnished by the association and questionable deference paid by the prosecutors. Marr's most compelling testimony involved the bullet found in Brady Paul's arm (one of three that struck him). He confidently claimed it could not have been fired by the gun carried by Private Ernest Moore, undercutting the friendly fire theory.

Scientific evidence aside, one of the most gripping testimonies came from the *Youngstown Vindicator* reporter Ella Kerber Resch, who initially received a handwritten manuscript containing a sensationalized account of Irene's life story. Published in serial format in the Ohio newspaper, the autobiographical tale revealed details that served only to bolster the prosecution's characterization of Irene as a cold-blooded trigger woman. Irene would later admit that she'd agreed to its publication because she needed the money for Donnie. It was obvious, though, that the story had been edited and supplemented by someone with expertise in attracting readership, but Resch initially would not divulge the origin of the material. She took the witness stand only after spending several days in jail for refusing to reveal her source for the manuscript. Before officially releasing her from custody, Judge Hildebrand remarked on her change of attitude and threw one last dig before excusing her. "If you didn't know it before," he said, "it is time you are learning that you must answer questions put to you by the court." Resch's journalistic resolve suffered yet another ignominy in 1973 when a report by the US House of Representatives' Judiciary Committee remembered her as one of only four reporters to yield to judicial pressure to reveal their sources.

In all, more than fifty prosecution witnesses testified that Irene either killed Brady Paul, was a participant in the shootout that precipitated his death, or committed some other crime.

On Tuesday, March 18, 1930, the jury got its first, long look at Irene Schroeder. Her testimony immediately followed that of her lover, W. Glenn Dague. Lacking her usual cockiness, Irene took a cautious approach to Margiotti's questions, sometimes stumbling in her replies. She returned to the stand the following day and matter-of-factly admitted that she was the one who chose Wish Angert's store in Butler, Pennsylvania, as a target for a holdup.

When asked why she, brother Tom Crawford, and Glenn had come from West Virginia to Pennsylvania in the first place, Irene said, "We took a ride up there to see the country."

She played into Margiotti's hands when she admitted that the Butler robbery "thrilled me for fifteen minutes" and that holdups, in general, "tickled" her. This, of course, led the prosecutor to ask if the shooting of Corporal Brady Paul also gave her a thrill.

"No," Irene replied. "It was all over then."

Even with her own life on the line, as she had done so many times before, Irene attempted to shield Glenn from blame. She denied that Glenn had even fired his weapon at Corporal Paul. She admitted firing her own gun, point-blank, toward Paul's chest but explained she had done so only because she believed Paul was going to shoot Glenn.

Once the shootout with Corporal Paul and Private Moore was reconstructed, Margiotti took Irene on a cross-country tour of her criminal activities, ending in Arizona. In one of her most bizarre acts of courtroom theater, Irene testified that—while taking cover from the posse in the Estrella Mountains—she gazed up at the sky and saw clouds that seemed to be sending messages. One cloud "looked like the face of Jesus," she said. Another looked like an ostrich. She remembered Glenn telling her it was a sign that they should go to Africa and preach the word of Christ. If Irene meant the testimony to be sympathetic, she badly misread the room. Members of the gallery, against Judge Hildebrand's admonitions, let loose an audible peal of laughter. But Irene wasn't done with her ludicrous proclamations, adding one last surprise. To Margiotti's question about her possible pregnancy, Irene replied, "Yes. I expect my baby in about four and a half months." It was one of Irene's more easily disputed lies.

Not to be outdone in the shock-and-awe department, Irene's defense team used this memorably outlandish day to finally announce their planned defense strategy. Irene, attorney Jarrett said, was pleading insanity. The prosecution vehemently objected, but the judge allowed Irene's lawyers to suggest a psychological justification for Irene's criminal career. Thanks to a severe head injury suffered at the age of ten, they explained, Irene possessed an irresistible impulse to steal, rob, and flee. As prosecutors furiously and repeatedly interrupted, Irene described to the jury the changes the accident made to her personality. She even managed to add that she'd tried to commit suicide several times. It was a naked play for sympathy and Irene's only chance to evade the death penalty.

In closing arguments, the defense attorneys doubled down on their efforts to both offer the jury an alternate version of the shootout and shock them into realizing what their possible death recommendation might mean. Thomas Dickey suggested it was Private Ernest Moore who had really caused Corporal Brady Paul's death by crouching, cowering, and hiding during the gun battle before finally firing wildly and without regard for his fellow officer's safety. Benjamin Jarrett took the jury through each excruciating step of an execution, from the time the prisoner left her cell to the point when several thousand volts charged through her body, literally boiling her blood. It was the only time the seemingly impenetrable Irene broke down.

Margiotti used his closing arguments to focus squarely on Irene, even going so far as to call the twenty-one-year-old high school dropout the "master mind of a criminal organization."

The prosecution rested on March 21, and the jury received the case at 6:45 that evening. Less than three hours later, they notified the bailiff that they'd reached a verdict.

"In the case of the Commonwealth versus Irene Schroeder, alias Irene Shrader, how do you find?" asked Judge Hildebrand.

"We find the defendant guilty of murder of the first degree," said jury foreman F. J. Rodgers, "and we fix the penalty at death."

There was a slight, silent pause as courtroom observers processed the verdict. Irene's family's loud and mournful sobs then fractured the stillness.

Irene accepted the verdict with her characteristic stoic attitude and stony expression. She told her sisters to hush. Irene's defense attorneys were already planning to appeal.

W. Glenn Dague's trial was far less dramatic than Irene's. The shock had already been absorbed; the story had already been told. Glenn's defense was fairly simple compared to Irene's. He was, attorneys Dickey and Jarrett insisted, a hapless man dominated by his young lover and enticed into committing crimes with her. The strategy not only contradicted their arguments in Irene's trial, but it was also a spectacular failure. Ten days later, Glenn, too, received a verdict of guilty with a recommended penalty of death.

On July 7, 1930, Judge Hildebrand heard defense counsels' arguments for the granting of a new trial for both Irene and Glenn. A month later, he ruled against their petition and sentenced both to die in the electric chair at a date selected by the governor. With this decision, the case was out of Lawrence County's hands. But while the legal maneuvers may have concluded at the county level, the defense had twenty-one days to appeal Hildebrand's decision to the Pennsylvania Superior Court. On November 24, it too upheld the convictions of both Irene and Glenn. Three weeks later, Governor Fisher granted a stay of execution to enable the Pennsylvania Board of Pardons to hear arguments for the commutation of the death sentences. Since the board didn't meet during the month of January, it was clear the legal wrangling would continue into 1931, when a new administration would take charge. On November 4, 1930, Gifford Pinchot won his bid for his second, although non-consecutive, term as governor. Pinchot's Board of Pardons was Irene's and Glenn's only hope to avoid execution. That hope was dashed on February 13, 1931, when the board refused to recommend commutation of the couple's death sentences to life imprisonment. Their execution date was set for February 23. Due to the board's refusal to recommend commutation, Governor Pinchot had the authority to grant a temporary stay of execution, but he could not grant clemency.

A week later, as if Donnie had not been exploited and punished enough, Irene's father brought him and several other relatives to Harrisburg to meet with Governor Pinchot. In a conversation that lasted only minutes, they begged for Irene's life. Pinchot explained that his hands had been tied by the pardon board, but it is doubtful that Donnie understood this legal nuance. It's equally doubtful that Pinchot was unmoved by the meeting and the little boy's plaintive request for help. Still, he had no choice but to decline the child's request to save his mother.

February 20 was the last night that Irene spent in the Lawrence County jail. It was, by all accounts, a peculiarly peaceful evening. Joseph Crawford brought Donnie to Irene's cell to say goodbye. "I am going to die," she told the child, "but I am not afraid. Be a good boy."

Both Irene and Glenn spent time writing their final wishes. Irene asked that the two be buried together with joint services. She spent the rest of the evening singing hymns.

Executions by hanging began in the Commonwealth of Pennsylvania in the 1600s. The individual counties determined and implemented these punishments until 1913, when they moved to state jurisdiction. The method of execution also changed that year. Hanging was replaced by electrocution.

Unlike hanging, which requires only quick and temporary wooden gallows and sturdy rope, electrocution requires special equipment, not to mention a reliably massive electrical current. To meet these requirements, the Pennsylvania Department of Corrections in 1912 began construction on the Rockview state correctional facility in Centre County. Within the grounds of this facility is housed Pennsylvania's death chamber. Prisoners sentenced to die by electrocution are only brought to Rockview in the few days preceding their execution. Such was the case for Irene and Glenn.

Early on the morning of February 21, Lawrence County guards awoke the doomed woman and man to eat and prepare for the nearly 200-mile car ride to Rockview. Even as they headed toward the execution chamber, some hoped for a last-minute reprieve. The Pennsylvania Prison Society (founded in 1787 as the Philadelphia Society for Alleviating the Miseries of Public Prisons) attempted to obtain a thirty-day stay of execution so that Irene could receive a full "psychopathic evaluation." If he read the request, Governor Pinchot did not honor it.

Hitchhiker and criminal ally Vernon Ackerman also tried to save his former accomplices' lives, though by less honest means. He told a wildly melodramatic story about Irene's brother, Tom Crawford. Crawford, said Ackerman, died in his arms in January 1930 after a shootout with police, but before drawing his last breath, he confessed to the killing of Corporal Brady. This well-intended but fanciful ploy was dismissed at the time and irrefutably proven untrue several years later when Tom Crawford was killed in yet another shootout with the police.

Rockview's Warden Stanley described both Irene and Glenn as being in good spirits the day before their execution, adding that they both ate their meals heartily. Meanwhile, eager reporters overran the nearby town of

Bellefonte. Larger news organizations monopolized telephone lines, and a dedicated connection was created between the facility and Harrisburg in the event Governor Pinchot called with a last-minute reprieve.

Also arriving in advance of the day of execution was Robert Elliott. Elliott was a celebrity in his own morbid way. As the official executioner for New York and Pennsylvania, he'd thrown the switch on a number of notorious criminals, including convicted Lindbergh baby kidnapper Bruno Hauptmann and anarchists Sacco and Vanzetti.

There would be twelve witnesses to the executions, half of whom would be reporters. They would not sit behind glass in an adjoining room. Instead, they would be seated within the death chamber itself. Only a rope divided these spectators from the prisoners and the electric chair into which they would be strapped.

It was the state's policy that executions be held at 7:00 a.m. In the rare event where two people were scheduled to die on the same day, the order of execution was determined by death warrant number. The inmate with the lowest numbered warrant went first.

Glenn's warrant number was 262. Irene's was 261.

Irene was roused at 5:30 a.m. on February 23, 1931. She was served breakfast before changing into a gray smock with white collar and sleeves and a pair of black slippers. A small bald spot was shaved onto the back of her head to better accept the electrical connection. She had just started to sing gospel hymns when the guards arrived at her cell to lead her to the death chamber.

Irene was taken down an empty corridor. She was stopped at a green door—the entrance into the room in which the witnesses, warden, and the electric chair waited. The prison reverend and the matron followed behind Irene. The matron silently cried as Irene seated herself in the chair and adjusted her small posture.

Guards secured her ankles, wrists, neck, and waist with leather straps before placing a leather mask on her face.

Robert Elliott worked the electric chair's controls like a conductor leading a mad orchestra. On first contact, 2,000 volts ripped through her body for three full seconds. This quick jolt was meant to be a humane way to rapidly cease organ function and eliminate the sensation of additional pain. The second contact, at 500 volts, lasted fifty-seven seconds. Elliott then once again blasted 2,000 volts through Irene, followed by another fifty-seven seconds at 500 volts. One last contact delivered 2,000 more volts for a final three seconds.

Irene had stepped inside the execution chamber at 7:01. At 7:05, she was officially declared dead. The only evidence of her horrific end was the little black slipper that slid off of her foot and onto the floor during her electrocution.

Eight minutes after Irene's body was rolled into the autopsy room, Glenn's arrived beside her.

Glenn's body went home to his family plot. The wife he'd abandoned for Irene petitioned the government for a headstone, based on Glenn's war service. The request was granted, and the stone, "for the unmarked grave of a World War soldier," was shipped to her on June 29, 1931.

On June 19, 1931, community organizers formalized plans to erect a monument to Corporal Brady Paul, near the spot on the Butler-New Castle Highway where he was shot. According to current Lawrence County Commissioner Dan Vogler, it was erected on Thursday, November 5, 1931.

"For the past decade, Lawrence County President Judge Dominick Motto and I have laid a wreath at this monument each December 27 at noon in honor of Corporal Paul's sacrifice," Vogler says. "Over the past few years, a growing number of law enforcement officials have joined us for this brief ceremony. As one police officer said to me on a cold, icy day, 'If Brady Paul could make the ultimate sacrifice at this location, the least I can do is come out to show my respect.'"

Irene's body was shipped by train to Ohio, where she was buried in an unmarked grave beside her mother. On the journey, an unscrupulous trainman pried open the makeshift coffin and allowed several friends to take a peek at her corpse.

Shortly after her execution, the Pennsylvania legislature—as it had done several times previously—considered abolishing the death penalty. One editor went so far as to predict that the first state-sponsored electrocution of a woman would crystalize public sentiment against the death penalty. It did not. Death by execution is still a punishment in the Keystone State, but one thing has changed since Irene Schroeder became the first woman to be electrocuted here. In 1990, electrocution was abolished in favor of lethal injection.

ABOUT THE AUTHOR

Stephanie Hoover is an author and researcher specializing in Pennsylvania true crime, myths, and legends, as well as its nineteenth-century Spiritualism movement. Her television work includes an appearance on Travel Channel's *Dead Files,* research for popular genealogy shows including *Who Do You Think You Are?,* and research for a SyFy Channel special on the Kecksburg, Pennsylvania, UFO incident. Stephanie is a member of the Authors Guild. She lives in Central Pennsylvania. Learn more at StephanieHoover.com.